2005 SUPPLEMENT

CASES AND MATERIALS

CONSTITUTIONAL LAW

TWELFTH EDITION

by

WILLIAM COHEN
C. Wendell and Edith M. Carlsmith
Professor Emeritus, Stanford Law School

JONATHAN D. VARAT
Professor of Law
University of California, Los Angeles

VIKRAM AMAR
Professor of Law
University of California, Hastings College of the Law

FOUNDATION PRESS
NEW YORK, NEW YORK
2005

THOMSON
WEST

395 Hudson Street
New York, NY 10014
Phone Toll Free 1–877–888–1330
Fax (212) 367–6799
fdpress.com
Printed in the United States of America

ISBN 1–58778–941–8

TEXT IS PRINTED ON 10% POST CONSUMER RECYCLED PAPER

PREFACE

On July 1, 2005, Justice O'Connor sent a letter to President George W. Bush informing him of her "decision to retire from my position as an associate justice of the Supreme Court of the United States, effective upon the nomination and confirmation of my successor."

*

TABLE OF CONTENTS
(**Bold** Indicates Principal Cases)

CHAPTER 10 THE EQUAL PROTECTION CLAUSE AND THE REVIEW OF THE REASONABLENESS OF LEGISLATION

CHAPTER 11 DEFINING THE SCOPE OF "LIBERTY" AND "PROPERTY" PROTECTED BY THE DUE PROCESS CLAUSE—THE PROCEDURAL DUE PROCESS CASES

TABLE OF CASES

Principal cases are in bold type. Non-principal cases are in roman type. References are to Pages.

*

2005 SUPPLEMENT

CONSTITUTIONAL LAW

*

PART II

Allocation of Governmental Powers: The Nation and the States; The President, The Congress, and The Courts

CHAPTER 4

The Scope of National Power

SECTION 3. The Scope of National Power Today

A. The Commerce Power

Page 192. Add before Pierce County v. Guillen:

Gonzales v. Raich

___ U.S. ___, 125 S.Ct. 2195, ___ L.Ed.2d ___ (2005).

Justice Stevens delivered the opinion of the Court.

California is one of at least nine States that authorize the use of marijuana for medicinal purposes. The question presented in this case is whether the power vested in Congress by Article I, § 8, of the Constitution "[t]o make all Laws which shall be necessary and proper for carrying into Execution" its authority to "regulate Commerce with foreign Nations, and among the several States" includes the power to prohibit the local cultivation and use of marijuana in compliance with California law.

I

. . . In 1996, California voters passed Proposition 215, now codified as the Compassionate Use Act of 1996. The proposition was designed to ensure that "seriously ill" residents of the State have access to marijuana for medical purposes, and to encourage Federal and State Governments to take steps towards ensuring the safe and affordable distribution of the drug to patients in need. The Act creates an exemption from criminal prosecution for physicians, as well as for patients and primary caregivers who possess or cultivate marijuana for medicinal purposes with the recommendation or approval of a physician. . . .

Respondents Angel Raich and Diane Monson are . . . being treated by licensed, board-certified family practitioners, who have concluded, after prescribing a host of conventional medicines to treat respondents' conditions and to alleviate their associated symptoms, that marijuana is the only drug available that provides effective treatment. Both women have been using marijuana as a medication for several years pursuant to their doctors' recommendation, and both rely heavily on cannabis to function on a daily basis. . . .

Respondent Monson cultivates her own marijuana, and ingests the drug in a variety of ways including smoking and using a vaporizer. Respondent Raich, by contrast, is unable to cultivate her own, and thus relies on two caregivers. . . .

On August 15, 2002, county deputy sheriffs and agents from the federal Drug Enforcement Administration (DEA) came to Monson's home. After a thorough investigation, the county officials concluded that her use of marijuana was entirely lawful as a matter of California law. Nevertheless, after a 3-hour standoff, the federal agents seized and destroyed all six of her cannabis plants.

Respondents thereafter brought this action against the Attorney General of the United States and the head of the DEA seeking injunctive and declaratory relief prohibiting the enforcement of the federal Controlled Substances Act (CSA) [21 U.S.C. § 801 *et. seq.*] . . . to the extent it prevents them from possessing, obtaining, or manufacturing cannabis for their personal medical use. . . . Respondents claimed [among other things] that enforcing the CSA against them would violate the Commerce Clause. . . .

. . .

[The Ninth Circuit reversed the district court's denial of respondents' motion for a preliminary injunction.] The Court of Appeals distinguished prior Circuit cases upholding the CSA in the face of Commerce Clause challenges by focusing on what it deemed to be the "*separate and distinct class of activities*" at issue in this case: "the intrastate, noncommercial cultivation and possession of cannabis for personal medical purposes as recommended by a patient's physician pursuant to valid California state law." ...

. . .

The obvious importance of the case prompted our grant of certiorari.... Well-settled law controls our ... [resolution of this case]. The CSA is a valid exercise of federal power, even as applied to the troubling facts of this case. We accordingly vacate the judgment of the Court of Appeals.

II

. . .

... [A]s early as 1906 Congress enacted federal legislation imposing labeling regulations on medications and prohibiting the manufacture or shipment of any adulterated or misbranded drug traveling in interstate commerce....

Marijuana itself was not significantly regulated by the Federal Government until 1937 when accounts of marijuana's addictive qualities and physiological effects, paired with dissatisfaction with enforcement efforts at state and local levels, prompted Congress to pass the Marihuana Tax Act ... [which] did not outlaw the possession or sale of marijuana outright. Rather, it imposed registration and reporting requirements for all individuals importing, producing, selling, or dealing in marijuana, and required the payment of annual taxes in addition to transfer taxes whenever the drug changed hands....

... [I]n 1970, after declaration of the national "war on drugs," federal drug policy underwent a significant transformation.... [Ultimately, that year] ..., prompted by a perceived need to consolidate the growing number of piecemeal drug laws and to enhance federal drug enforcement powers, Congress enacted the Comprehensive Drug Abuse Prevention and Control Act.

Title II of that Act, the CSA, repealed most of the earlier antidrug laws in favor of a comprehensive regime to combat the international and interstate traffic in illicit drugs. The main objectives of the CSA were to conquer drug abuse and to control the legitimate and illegitimate traffic in controlled substances.[20] Congress was particularly concerned with the need to prevent the diversion of drugs from legitimate to illicit channels.

20. In particular, Congress made the following findings:

"(1) Many of the drugs included within this subchapter have a useful and legitimate medical purpose and are necessary to maintain the health and general welfare of the American people.

"(2) The illegal importation, manufacture, distribution, and possession and improper use of controlled substances have a substantial and detrimental effect on the health and general welfare of the American people.

"(3) A major portion of the traffic in controlled substances flows through interstate and foreign commerce. Incidents of the traffic which are not an integral part of the interstate or foreign flow, such as manufacture, local distribution, and possession, nonetheless have a substantial and direct effect upon interstate commerce because—

"(A) after manufacture, many controlled substances are transported in interstate commerce,

"(B) controlled substances distributed locally usually have been transported in

To effectuate these goals, Congress devised a closed regulatory system making it unlawful to manufacture, distribute, dispense, or possess any controlled substance except in a manner authorized by the CSA. 21 U.S.C. §§ 841(a)(1), 844(a). The CSA categorizes all controlled substances into five schedules. § 812. The drugs are grouped together based on their accepted medical uses, the potential for abuse, and their psychological and physical effects on the body.... Each schedule is associated with a distinct set of controls regarding the manufacture, distribution, and use of the substances listed therein.... The CSA and its implementing regulations set forth strict requirements regarding registration, labeling and packaging, production quotas, drug security, and recordkeeping....

In enacting the CSA, Congress classified marijuana as a Schedule I drug. 21 U.S.C. § 812(c).... Schedule I drugs are categorized as such because of their high potential for abuse, lack of any accepted medical use, and absence of any accepted safety for use in medically supervised treatment. § 812(b)(1).... By classifying marijuana as a Schedule I drug, as opposed to listing it on a lesser schedule, the manufacture, distribution, or possession of marijuana became a criminal offense, with the sole exception being use of the drug as part of a Food and Drug Administration pre-approved research study. §§ 823(f), 841(a)(1), 844(a); see also United States v. Oakland Cannibis Buyers' Cooperative, 532 U.S. 483, 490 (2001).

... Despite considerable efforts to reschedule marijuana, it remains a Schedule I drug.

III

Respondents ... do not dispute that passage of the CSA, as part of the Comprehensive Drug Abuse Prevention and Control Act, was well within Congress' commerce power.... Nor do they contend that any provision or section of the CSA amounts to an unconstitutional exercise of congressional authority. Rather, respondents' challenge is actually quite limited; they argue that the CSA's categorical prohibition of the manufacture and possession of marijuana as applied to the intrastate manufacture and possession of marijuana for medical purposes pursuant to California law exceeds Congress' authority under the Commerce Clause.

In assessing the validity of congressional regulation, none of our Commerce Clause cases can be viewed in isolation. As charted in considerable detail in United States v. Lopez [514 U.S. 549 (1995)], our understanding of the reach of

interstate commerce immediately before their distribution, and

"(C) controlled substances possessed commonly flow through interstate commerce immediately prior to such possession.

"(4) Local distribution and possession of controlled substances contribute to swelling the interstate traffic in such substances.

"(5) Controlled substances manufactured and distributed intrastate cannot be differentiated from controlled substances manufactured and distributed interstate. Thus, it is not feasible to distinguish, in terms of controls, between controlled substances manufactured and distributed interstate and controlled substances manufactured and distributed intrastate.

"(6) Federal control of the intrastate incidents of the traffic in controlled substances is essential to the effective control of the interstate incidents of such traffic." 21 U.S.C. §§ 801(1)–(6).

the Commerce Clause, as well as Congress' assertion of authority thereunder, has evolved over time....

. . .

Our case law firmly establishes Congress' power to regulate purely local activities that are part of an economic "class of activities" that have a substantial effect on interstate commerce.... As we stated in [Wickard v. Filburn, 317 U.S. 111, 125], "even if appellee's activity be local and though it may not be regarded as commerce, it may still, whatever its nature, be reached by Congress if it exerts a substantial economic effect on interstate commerce." ... We have never required Congress to legislate with scientific exactitude. When Congress decides that the " 'total incidence' " of a practice poses a threat to a national market, it may regulate the entire class.... In this vein, we have reiterated that when " 'a general regulatory statute bears a substantial relation to commerce, the *de minimis* character of individual instances arising under that statute is of no consequence.' " ...

Our decision in *Wickard* ... is of particular relevance. In *Wickard*, we upheld the application of regulations promulgated under the Agricultural Adjustment Act [AAA] of 1938 ... which were designed to control the volume of wheat moving in interstate and foreign commerce in order to avoid surpluses and consequent abnormally low prices. The regulations established an allotment of 11.1 acres for Filburn's 1941 wheat crop, but he sowed 23 acres, intending to use the excess by consuming it on his own farm. Filburn argued that even though we had sustained Congress' power to regulate the production of goods for commerce, that power did not authorize "federal regulation [of] production not intended in any part for commerce but wholly for consumption on the farm." *Wickard*, 317 U.S. at 188. Justice Jackson's opinion for a unanimous Court rejected this submission. He wrote:

> "The effect of the statute before us is to restrict the amount which may be produced for market and the extent as well to which one may forestall resort to the market by producing to meet his own needs. That appellee's own contribution to the demand for wheat may be trivial by itself is not enough to remove him from the scope of federal regulation where, as here, his contribution, taken together with that of many others similarly situated, is far from trivial." *Id.*, at 127–128.

Wickard thus establishes that Congress can regulate purely intrastate activity that is not itself "commercial," in that it is not produced for sale, if it concludes that failure to regulate that class of activity would undercut the regulation of the interstate market in that commodity.

The similarities between this case and *Wickard* are striking. Like the farmer in *Wickard*, respondents are cultivating, for home consumption, a fungible commodity for which there is an established, albeit illegal, interstate market. Just as the Agricultural Adjustment Act was designed "to control the volume [of wheat] moving in interstate and foreign commerce in order to avoid surpluses ... " and consequently control the market price ... a primary purpose of the CSA is to control the supply and demand of controlled substances in both lawful and unlawful drug markets. See [n. 20] *supra*. In *Wickard*, we had no difficulty concluding that Congress had a rational basis for believing that, when viewed in the aggregate, leaving home-consumed wheat outside the regulatory scheme would have a substantial influence on price and market conditions. Here too, Congress had a rational basis for concluding that leaving home-consumed marijuana outside federal control would similarly affect price and market conditions.

More concretely, one concern prompting inclusion of wheat grown for home consumption in the 1938 Act was that rising market prices could draw such wheat into the interstate market, resulting in lower market prices.... The parallel concern making it appropriate to include marijuana grown for home consumption in the CSA is the likelihood that the high demand in the interstate market will draw such marijuana into that market.... In both cases, the regulation is squarely within Congress' commerce power because production of the commodity meant for home consumption, be it wheat or marijuana, has a substantial effect on supply and demand in the national market for that commodity.[29]

Nonetheless, respondents suggest that *Wickard* differs from this case in three respects: (1) the Agricultural Adjustment Act, unlike the CSA, exempted small farming operations; (2) *Wickard* involved a "quintessential economic activity"—a commercial farm—whereas respondents do not sell marijuana; and (3) the *Wickard* record made it clear that the aggregate production of wheat for use on farms had a significant impact on market prices. Those differences, though factually accurate, do not diminish the precedential force of this Court's reasoning.

The fact that ... [Filburn's] own impact on the market was "trivial by itself" was not a sufficient reason for removing him from the scope of federal regulation.... That the Secretary of Agriculture elected to exempt even smaller farms from regulation does not speak to his power to regulate all those whose aggregated production was significant, nor did that fact play any role in the Court's analysis. Moreover, even though ... [Filburn] was indeed a commercial farmer, the activity he was engaged in—the cultivation of wheat for home consumption—was not treated by the Court as part of his commercial farming operation. And while it is true that the record in the *Wickard* case itself established the causal connection between the production for local use and the national market, we have before us findings by Congress to the same effect.

Findings in the introductory sections of the CSA explain why Congress deemed it appropriate to encompass local activities within the scope of the CSA. See n. 20, *supra*.... Respondents nonetheless insist that the CSA cannot be constitutionally applied to their activities because Congress did not make a specific finding that the intrastate cultivation and possession of marijuana for medical purposes based on the recommendation of a physician would substantially affect the larger interstate marijuana market. Be that as it may, we have never required Congress to make particularized findings in order to legislate, see *Lopez*, 514 U.S. at 562, Perez [v. United States], 402 U.S. at 156, absent a special concern such as the protection of free speech.... While congressional

29. To be sure, the wheat market is a lawful market that Congress sought to protect and stabilize, whereas the marijuana market is an unlawful market that Congress sought to eradicate. This difference, however, is of no constitutional import. It has long been settled that Congress' power to regulate commerce includes the power to prohibit commerce in a particular commodity....

findings are certainly helpful in reviewing the substance of a congressional statutory scheme, particularly when the connection to commerce is not self-evident, and while we will consider congressional findings in our analysis when they are available, the absence of particularized findings does not call into question Congress' authority to legislate.

In assessing the scope of Congress' authority under the Commerce Clause, we stress that the task before us is a modest one. We need not determine whether respondents' activities, taken in the aggregate, substantially affect interstate commerce in fact, but only whether a "rational basis" exists for so concluding. *Lopez*, 514 U.S. at 557 .... Given the enforcement difficulties that attend distinguishing between marijuana cultivated locally and marijuana grown elsewhere ... and concerns about diversion into illicit channels, ... we have no difficulty concluding that Congress had a rational basis for believing that failure to regulate the intrastate manufacture and possession of marijuana would leave a gaping hole in the CSA. Thus, as in *Wickard*, when it enacted comprehensive legislation to regulate the interstate market in a fungible commodity, Congress was acting well within its authority to "make all Laws which shall be necessary and proper" to "regulate Commerce ... among the several States." U.S. Const., Art. I, § 8. That the regulation ensnares some purely intrastate activity is of no moment. As we have done many times before, we refuse to excise individual components of that larger scheme.

IV

To support their contrary submission, respondents rely heavily on two of our more recent Commerce Clause cases. In their myopic focus, they overlook the larger context of modern-era Commerce Clause jurisprudence preserved by those cases. Moreover, even in the narrow prism of respondents' creation, they read those cases far too broadly.

Those two cases, of course, are *Lopez* ... and [United States v. Morrison, 529 U.S 598 (2000)]. As an initial matter, the statutory challenges at issue in those cases were markedly different from the challenge respondents pursue in the case at hand. Here, respondents ask us to excise individual applications of a concededly valid statutory scheme. In contrast, in both *Lopez* and *Morrison*, the parties asserted that a particular statute or provision fell outside Congress' commerce power in its entirety. This distinction is pivotal for we have often reiterated that "[w]here the class of activities is regulated and that class is within the reach of federal power, the courts have no power 'to excise, as trivial, individual instances' of the class." ...

At issue in *Lopez* ... was the validity of the Gun-Free School Zones Act of 1990, which was a brief, single-subject statute making it a crime for an individual to possess a gun in a school zone.... Distinguishing our earlier cases holding that comprehensive regulatory statutes may be validly applied to local conduct that does not, when viewed in isolation, have a significant impact on interstate commerce, we held the statute invalid. We explained:

> "Section 922(q) [, the Act,] is a criminal statute that by its terms has nothing to do with 'commerce' or any sort of economic enterprise, however broadly one might define those terms. Section 922(q) is not an essential part of a larger regulation of economic activity, in which the regulatory scheme could be undercut unless the intrastate activity were regulated. It

cannot, therefore, be sustained under our cases upholding regulations of activities that arise out of or are connected with a commercial transaction, which viewed in the aggregate, substantially affects interstate commerce." 514 U.S. at 561.

The statutory scheme [here] is at the opposite end of the regulatory spectrum. [T]he CSA . . . was a lengthy and detailed statute creating a comprehensive framework for regulating the production, distribution, and possession of five classes of "controlled substances." . . .

. . . [The] classification [of marijuana as a Schedule I substance], unlike the discrete prohibition established by the Gun-Free School Zones Act of 1990, was merely one of many "essential part[s] of a larger regulation of economic activity, in which the regulatory scheme could be undercut unless the intrastate activity were regulated." *Lopez*, 514 U.S. at 561.[34] Our opinion in *Lopez* casts no doubt on the validity of such a program.

Nor does this Court's holding in *Morrison*. . . . The Violence Against Women Act of 1994 . . . created a federal civil remedy for the victims of gender-motivated crimes of violence. . . . The remedy was enforceable in both state and federal courts, and generally depended on proof of the violation of a state law. Despite congressional findings that such crimes had an adverse impact on interstate commerce, we held the statute unconstitutional because, like the statute in *Lopez*, it did not regulate economic activity. We concluded that "the noneconomic, criminal nature of the conduct at issue was central to our decision" in *Lopez*, and that our prior cases had identified a clear pattern of analysis: " 'Where economic activity substantially affects interstate commerce, legislation regulating that activity will be sustained.' " . . .

Unlike those at issue in *Lopez* and *Morrison*, the activities regulated by the CSA are quintessentially economic. "Economics" refers to "the production, distribution, and consumption of commodities." Webster's Third New International Dictionary 720 (1966). The CSA is a statute that regulates the production, distribution, and consumption of commodities for which there is an established, and lucrative, interstate market. Prohibiting the intrastate possession or manufacture of an article of commerce is a rational (and commonly utilized) means of regulating commerce in that product. . . .

The Court of Appeals was able to conclude otherwise only by isolating a "separate and distinct" class of activities that it held to be beyond the reach of federal power, defined as "the intrastate, noncommercial cultivation, possession and use of marijuana for personal medical purposes on the advice of a physician and in accordance with state law." . . . The court characterized this class as "different in kind from drug trafficking." . . . The differences between the members of a class so defined and the principal traffickers in Schedule I substances might be sufficient to justify a policy decision exempting the narrower class from the coverage of the CSA. The question, however, is whether Congress' contrary policy judgment, *i.e.*, its decision to include this

34. The principal dissent asserts that by "[s]eizing upon our language in *Lopez*", i.e., giving effect to our well-established case law, Congress will now have an incentive to legislate broadly. Even putting aside the political checks that would generally curb Congress' power to enact a broad and comprehensive scheme for the purpose of targeting purely local activity, there is no suggestion that the CSA constitutes the type of "evasive" legislation the dissent fears, nor could such an argument plausibly be made. . . .

narrower "class of activities" within the larger regulatory scheme, was constitutionally deficient. We have no difficulty concluding that Congress acted rationally....

. . .

... [It cannot] serve as an "objective marke[r]" or "objective facto[r]" to arbitrarily narrow the relevant class as the dissenters suggest.... More fundamentally, if, as the principal dissent contends, the personal cultivation, possession, and use of marijuana for medicinal purposes is beyond the " 'outer limits' of Congress' Commerce Clause authority," ... it must also be true that such personal use of marijuana (or any other homegrown drug) for recreational purposes is also beyond those " 'outer limits,' " whether or not a State elects to authorize or even regulate such use.... One need not have a degree in economics to understand why a nationwide exemption for the vast quantity of marijuana (or other drugs) locally cultivated for personal use (which presumably would include use by friends, neighbors, and family members) may have a substantial impact on the interstate market for this extraordinarily popular substance....

Second, limiting the activity to marijuana possession and cultivation "in accordance with state law" cannot serve to place respondents' activities beyond congressional reach. The Supremacy Clause unambiguously provides that if there is any conflict between federal and state law, federal law shall prevail....

. . .

V

... The case is remanded for further proceedings consistent with this opinion....

Justice Scalia, concurring in the judgment.

I agree with the Court's holding that the Controlled Substances Act (CSA) may validly be applied to respondents' cultivation, distribution, and possession of marijuana for personal, medicinal use. I write separately because my understanding of the doctrinal foundation on which that holding rests is, if not inconsistent with that of the Court, at least more nuanced.

. . .

I

. . .

As we implicitly acknowledged in *Lopez* ... , Congress's authority to enact laws necessary and proper for the regulation of interstate commerce is not limited to laws directed against economic activities that have a substantial effect on interstate commerce. Though the conduct in *Lopez* was not economic, the Court nevertheless recognized that it could be regulated as "an essential part of a larger regulation of economic activity, in which the regulatory scheme could be undercut unless the intrastate activity were regulated." ... This statement referred to those cases permitting the regulation of intrastate activities "which in a substantial way interfere with or obstruct the exercise of the granted power." . . .

. . . The regulation of an intrastate activity may be essential to a comprehensive regulation of interstate commerce even though the intrastate activity does not itself "substantially affect" interstate commerce. Moreover, as the passage from *Lopez* quoted above suggests, Congress may regulate even noneconomic local activity if that regulation is a necessary part of a more general regulation of interstate commerce. . . . The relevant question is simply whether the means chosen are "reasonably adapted" to the attainment of a legitimate end under the commerce power. . . .

. . .

II

Today's principal dissent objects that, by permitting Congress to regulate activities necessary to effective interstate regulation, the Court reduces *Lopez* and *Morrison* to "little more than a drafting guide." . . . I think that criticism unjustified. Unlike the power to regulate activities that have a substantial effect on interstate commerce, the power to enact laws enabling effective regulation of interstate commerce can only be exercised in conjunction with congressional regulation of an interstate market, and it extends only to those measures necessary to make the interstate regulation effective. As *Lopez* itself states, and the Court affirms today, Congress may regulate noneconomic intrastate activities only where the failure to do so "could . . . undercut" its regulation of interstate commerce. . . . This is not a power that threatens to obliterate the line between "what is truly national and what is truly local." . . .

Neither . . . [*Lopez* nor *Morrison*] involved the power of Congress to exert control over intrastate activities in connection with a more comprehensive scheme of regulation; *Lopez* expressly disclaimed that it was such a case . . . and *Morrison* did not even discuss the possibility that it was. . . . To dismiss this distinction as "superficial and formalistic," . . . [as Justice O'Connor's dissent does] is to misunderstand the nature of the Necessary and Proper Clause, which empowers Congress to enact laws in effectuation of its enumerated powers that are not within its authority to enact in isolation. See McCulloch v. Maryland, 4 Wheat. 316, 421–244 (1819).

And there are other restraints upon the Necessary and Proper Clause authority. As Chief Justice Marshall wrote in *McCulloch* . . . , even when the end is constitutional and legitimate, the means must be "appropriate" and "plainly adapted" to that end. . . . Moreover, they may not be otherwise "prohibited" and must be "consistent with the letter and spirit of the constitution." . . . These phrases are not merely hortatory. For example, cases such as Printz v. United States, 521 U.S. 898 (1997) and New York v. United States, 505 U.S. 144 (1992), affirm that a law is not " 'proper for carrying into Execution the Commerce Clause' " "[w]hen [it] violates [a constitutional] principle of state sovereignty." . . .

III

The application of these principles to the case before us is straightforward. In the CSA, Congress has undertaken to extinguish the interstate market in

Schedule I controlled substances, including marijuana. The Commerce Clause unquestionably permits this. The power to regulate interstate commerce "extends not only to those regulations which aid, foster and protect the commerce, but embraces those which prohibit it." ... To effectuate its objective, Congress has prohibited almost all intrastate activities related to Schedule I substances—both economic activities (manufacture, distribution, possession with the intent to distribute) and noneconomic activities (simple possession).... That simple possession is a noneconomic activity is immaterial to whether it can be prohibited as a necessary part of a larger regulation....

... Not only is it impossible to distinguish "controlled substances manufactured and distributed intrastate" from "controlled substances manufactured and distributed interstate," but it hardly makes sense to speak in such terms. Drugs like marijuana are fungible commodities. As the Court explains, marijuana that is grown at home and possessed for personal use is never more than an instant from the interstate market—and this is so whether or not the possession is for medicinal use or lawful use under the laws of a particular State.[3] ... Congress need not accept on faith that state law will be effective in maintaining a strict division between a lawful market for "medical" marijuana and the more general marijuana market.... "To impose on [Congress] the necessity of resorting to means which it cannot control, which another government may furnish or withhold, would render its course precarious, the result of its measures uncertain, and create a dependence on other governments, which might disappoint its most important designs, and is incompatible with the language of the constitution." *McCulloch* ....

. . .

Justice O'Connor, with whom the Chief Justice and Justice Thomas join as to all but part III, dissenting.

. . .

This case exemplifies the role of States as laboratories. The States' core police powers have always included authority to define criminal law and to protect the health, safety, and welfare of their citizens.... Today the Court sanctions an application of the federal Controlled Substances Act that extinguishes ... [California's] experiment, without any proof that the personal cultivation, possession, and use of marijuana for medicinal purposes, if economic activity in the first place, has a substantial effect on interstate commerce and is therefore an appropriate subject of federal regulation. In so doing, the Court

3. The principal dissent claims that, if this is sufficient to sustain the regulation at issue in this case, then it should also have been sufficient to sustain the regulation at issue in [*Lopez*].... This claim founders upon the shoals of *Lopez* itself, which made clear that the statute there at issue was "not an essential part of a larger regulation of economic activity." ... On the dissent's view of things, that statement is inexplicable. Of course it is in addition difficult to imagine what intelligible scheme of regulation of the interstate market in guns could have as an appropriate means of effectuation the prohibition of guns within 1000 feet of schools (and nowhere else). The dissent [mentions] a federal law ... barring licensed dealers from selling guns to minors, ... but the relationship between the regulatory scheme of which [that statute] is a part (requiring all dealers in firearms that have traveled in interstate commerce to be licensed ...) and the statute at issue in *Lopez* approaches the nonexistent—which is doubtless why the Government did not attempt to justify the statute on the basis of that relationship.

announces a rule that gives Congress a perverse incentive to legislate broadly pursuant to the Commerce Clause—nestling questionable assertions of its authority into comprehensive regulatory schemes—rather than with precision. That rule and the result it produces in this case are irreconcilable with our decisions in [*Lopez* and *Morrison*]. Accordingly I dissent.

. . .

II

A

What is the relevant conduct subject to Commerce Clause analysis in this case? The Court takes its cues from Congress.... The Court's decision rests on two facts about the CSA: (1) Congress chose to enact a single statute providing a comprehensive prohibition on the production, distribution, and possession of all controlled substances, and (2) Congress did not distinguish between various forms of intrastate noncommercial cultivation, possession, and use of marijuana.... Today's decision suggests that the federal regulation of local activity is immune to Commerce Clause challenge because Congress chose to act with an ambitious, all-encompassing statute, rather than piecemeal. In my view, allowing Congress to set the terms of the constitutional debate in this way, i.e., by packaging regulation of local activity in broader schemes, is tantamount to removing meaningful limits on the Commerce Clause.

The Court's principal means of distinguishing *Lopez* from this case is to observe that the Gun-Free School Zones Act of 1990 was a "brief, single-subject statute," ... whereas the CSA is "a lengthy and detailed statute creating a comprehensive framework for regulating the production, distribution, and possession of five classes of 'controlled substances,' ".... Thus, according to the Court, it was possible in *Lopez* to evaluate in isolation the constitutionality of criminalizing local activity (there gun possession in school zones), whereas the local activity that the CSA targets (in this case cultivation and possession of marijuana for personal medicinal use) cannot be separated from the general drug control scheme of which it is a part.

Today's decision allows Congress to regulate intrastate activity without check, so long as there is some implication by legislative design that regulating intrastate activity is essential (and the Court appears to equate "essential" with "necessary") to the interstate regulatory scheme. Seizing upon our language in *Lopez* that the statute prohibiting gun possession in school zones was "not an essential part of a larger regulation of economic activity, in which the regulatory scheme could be undercut unless the intrastate activity were regulated," ... the Court appears to reason that the placement of local activity in a comprehensive scheme confirms that it is essential to that scheme.... If the Court is right, then *Lopez* stands for nothing more than a drafting guide: Congress should have described the relevant crime as "transfer or possession of a firearm anywhere in the nation"—thus including commercial and noncommercial activity, and clearly encompassing some activity with assuredly substantial effect on interstate commerce. Had it done so, the majority hints, we would have sustained its authority to regulate possession of firearms in school zones....

I cannot agree that our decision in *Lopez* contemplated such evasive or overbroad legislative strategies with approval. Until today, such arguments have been made only in dissent.... *Lopez* and *Morrison* did not indicate that the constitutionality of federal regulation depends on superficial and formalistic distinctions. Likewise I did not understand our discussion of the role of courts in enforcing outer limits of the Commerce Clause for the sake of maintaining the federalist balance our Constitution requires ... as a signal to Congress to enact legislation that is more extensive and more intrusive into the domain of state power. If the Court always defers to Congress as it does today, little may be left to the notion of enumerated powers.

The hard work for courts ... is to identify objective markers for confining the analysis in Commerce Clause cases. Here, respondents challenge the constitutionality of the CSA as applied to them and those similarly situated. I agree with the Court that we must look beyond respondents' own activities. Otherwise, individual litigants could always exempt themselves from Commerce Clause regulation merely by pointing to the obvious—that their personal activities do not have a substantial effect on interstate commerce.... The task is to identify a mode of analysis that allows Congress to regulate more than nothing (by declining to reduce each case to its litigants) and less than everything (by declining to let Congress set the terms of analysis). The analysis may not be the same in every case, for it depends on the regulatory scheme at issue and the federalism concerns implicated....

A number of objective markers are available to confine the scope of constitutional review here. Both federal and state legislation—including the CSA itself, the California Compassionate Use Act, and other state medical marijuana legislation—recognize that medical and nonmedical (i.e., recreational) uses of drugs are realistically distinct and can be segregated, and regulate them differently.... Moreover, because fundamental structural concerns about dual sovereignty animate our Commerce Clause cases, it is relevant that this case involves the interplay of federal and state regulation in areas of criminal law and social policy, where "States lay claim by right of history and expertise." ... California, like other States, has drawn on its reserved powers to distinguish the regulation of medicinal marijuana. To ascertain whether Congress' encroachment is constitutionally justified in this case, then, I would focus here on the personal cultivation, possession, and use of marijuana for medicinal purposes.

B

Having thus defined the relevant conduct, we must determine whether, under our precedents, the conduct is economic and, in the aggregate, substantially affects interstate commerce. Even if intrastate cultivation and possession of marijuana for one's own medicinal use can properly be characterized as economic, and I question whether it can, it has not been shown that such activity substantially affects interstate commerce. Similarly, it is neither self-evident nor demonstrated that regulating such activity is necessary to the interstate drug control scheme.

The Court's definition of economic activity is breathtaking. It defines as economic any activity involving the production, distribution, and consumption of commodities. And it appears to reason that when an interstate market for a commodity exists, regulating the intrastate manufacture or possession of that commodity is constitutional either because that intrastate activity is itself economic, or because regulating it is a rational part of regulating its market. Putting to one side the problem endemic to the Court's opinion—the shift in focus from the activity at issue in this case to the entirety of what the CSA regulates, see *Lopez* . . . ("depending on the level of generality, any activity can be looked upon as commercial")—the Court's definition of economic activity for purposes of Commerce Clause jurisprudence threatens to sweep all of productive human activity into federal regulatory reach.

. . . It will not do to say that Congress may regulate noncommercial activity simply because it may have an effect on the demand for commercial goods, or because the noncommercial endeavor can, in some sense, substitute for commercial activity. Most commercial goods or services have some sort of privately producible analogue. Home care substitutes for daycare. Charades games substitute for movie tickets. Backyard or windowsill gardening substitutes for going to the supermarket. To draw the line wherever private activity affects the demand for market goods is to draw no line at all, and to declare everything economic. We have already [explicitly] rejected [in *Lopez*] the result that would follow—a federal police power. . . .

In *Lopez* and *Morrison*, we suggested that economic activity usually relates directly to commercial activity. . . . The homegrown cultivation and personal possession and use of marijuana for medicinal purposes has no apparent commercial character. Everyone agrees that the marijuana at issue in this case was never in the stream of commerce, and neither were the supplies for growing it. (Marijuana is highly unusual among the substances subject to the CSA in that it can be cultivated without any materials that have traveled in interstate commerce.) *Lopez* makes clear that possession is not itself commercial activity. . . . And respondents have not come into possession by means of any commercial transaction; they have simply grown, in their own homes, marijuana for their own use, without acquiring, buying, selling, or bartering a thing of value. . . .

The Court suggests that *Wickard*, which we have identified as "perhaps the most far reaching example of Commerce Clause authority over intrastate activity," . . . established federal regulatory power over any home consumption of a commodity for which a national market exists. I disagree. In contrast to the CSA's limitless assertion of power, Congress provided an exemption within the AAA for small producers [in *Wickard*]. . . . *Wickard*, then, did not extend Commerce Clause authority to something as modest as the home cook's herb garden. This is not to say that Congress may never regulate small quantities of commodities possessed or produced for personal use, or to deny that it sometimes needs to enact a zero tolerance regime for such commodities. It is merely to say that *Wickard* did not hold or imply that small-scale production of commodities is always economic, and automatically within Congress' reach.

Even assuming that economic activity is at issue in this case, the Government has made no showing in fact that the possession and use of homegrown marijuana for medical purposes, in California or elsewhere, has a substantial effect on interstate commerce. Similarly, the Government has not shown that regulating such activity is necessary to an interstate regulatory scheme. . . .

That is why characterizing this as a case about the Necessary and Proper Clause does not change the analysis significantly.... [If it did] then we could have surmised in *Lopez* that guns in school zones are "never more than an instant from the interstate market" in guns already subject to extensive federal regulation, ... recast *Lopez* as a Necessary and Proper Clause case, and thereby upheld the Gun-Free School Zones Act of 1990. (According to the Court's and the concurrence's logic, for example, the *Lopez* [C]ourt should have reasoned that the prohibition on gun possession in school zones could be an appropriate means of effectuating a related [statutory] prohibition [that currently makes criminal the] ... "sell[ing]" or "deliver[ing]" firearms or ammunition to "any individual who the licensee knows or has reasonable cause to believe is less than eighteen years of age." ...)

There is simply no evidence that homegrown medicinal marijuana users constitute, in the aggregate, a sizable enough class to have a discernable, let alone substantial, impact on the national illicit drug market—or otherwise to threaten the CSA regime.... And here, in part because common sense suggests that medical marijuana users may be limited in number and that California's Compassionate Use Act and similar state legislation may well isolate activities relating to medicinal marijuana from the illicit market, the effect of those activities on interstate drug traffic is not self-evidently substantial.

In this regard, again, this case is readily distinguishable from *Wickard*. To decide whether the Secretary could regulate local wheat farming, the Court looked to "the actual effects of the activity in question upon interstate commerce." ... Critically, the Court was able to consider "actual effects" because the parties had "stipulated a summary of the economics of the wheat industry." ... With real numbers at hand, the *Wickard* Court could easily conclude that "a factor of such volume and variability as home-consumed wheat would have a substantial influence on price and market conditions" nationwide....

. . .

[The findings in the present case do not suffice.] In particular, the CSA's introductory declarations are too vague and unspecific to demonstrate that the federal statutory scheme will be undermined if Congress cannot exert power over individuals like respondents. The declarations are not even specific to marijuana ... The California Compassionate Use Act exempts from other state drug laws patients and their caregivers "who posses[s] or cultivat[e] marijuana for the personal medical purposes of the patient upon the written or oral recommendation of a physician" to treat a list of serious medical conditions.... The Act specifies that it should not be construed to supersede legislation prohibiting persons from engaging in acts dangerous to others, or to condone the diversion of marijuana for nonmedical purposes.... We generally assume States enforce their laws ... and have no reason to think otherwise here.

The Government has not overcome empirical doubt that the number of Californians engaged in personal cultivation, possession, and use of medical marijuana, or the amount of marijuana they produce, is enough to threaten the federal regime. Nor has it shown that Compassionate Use Act marijuana users have been or are realistically likely to be responsible for the drug's seeping into the market in a significant way....

III

. . . If I were a California citizen, I would not have voted for the medical marijuana ballot initiative; if I were a California legislator I would not have supported the Compassionate Use Act. But whatever the wisdom of California's experiment with medical marijuana, the federalism principles that have driven our Commerce Clause cases require that room for experiment be protected in this case. For these reasons I dissent.

Justice Thomas, dissenting.

. . . If Congress can regulate this under the Commerce Clause, then it can regulate virtually anything—and the Federal Government is no longer one of limited and enumerated powers.

. . .

II

B

. . .

. . . [I]t is implausible that this Court could set aside entire portions of the United States Code as outside Congress' power in *Lopez* and *Morrison*, but it cannot engage in the more restrained practice of invalidating particular applications of the CSA that are beyond Congress' power. This Court has regularly entertained as-applied challenges under constitutional provisions. . . . There is no reason why, when Congress exceeds the scope of commerce power, courts may not invalidate Congress' overreaching on a case-by-case basis. . . .

. . .

CHAPTER 6

The Scope of State Power

SECTION 5. Effect of Other Constitutional Provisions on State Regulatory Power

B. The Twenty-First Amendment

Page 371. Add before Brown-Forman Distillers Corp. v. New York State Liquor Authority:

GRANHOLM v. HEALD 125 S.Ct. 1885. The Court applied *Bacchus* to invalidate laws from Michigan and New York that allowed in-state, but not out-of-state, wineries to make sales to consumers directly, rather than through wholesale and retail distributors. Rejecting the argument made by the States that the Twenty-First Amendment authorized or permitted this kind of discrimination against interstate commerce, and that *Bacchus* ought to be overruled or limited, the five-member majority (Justices Kennedy, Scalia, Souter, Ginsburg and Breyer) read Section 2 of the Twenty-First Amendment as conferring upon states only that authority which Congress had tried to confer by passing the Wilson Act and the Webb-Kenyon Act prior to the adoption of the Twenty-First Amendment. Because nothing in either of these Acts purported to give states freedom to discriminate against out-of-state alcohol producers in violation of Commerce Clause norms, neither, said the Court, did Section 2 of the Amendment.

PART III

Government and the Individual: The Protection of Liberty and Property Under the Due Process and Equal Protection Clauses

CHAPTER 9

The Due Process, Contract, and Just Compensation Clauses and the Review of the Reasonableness of Legislation

SECTION 1. ECONOMIC REGULATORY LEGISLATION

C. THE JUST COMPENSATION CLAUSE OF THE FIFTH AMENDMENT—WHAT DOES IT ADD TO DUE PROCESS?

Page 552. Add at end of Introduction:

The Court in Kelo v. City of New London, 125 S.Ct. 2655 (2005), once more held the "public use" requirement satisfied, this time in a comprehensive opinion addressed exclusively to that question. Four Justices again dissented, although, unlike *Brown*, Justice Kennedy joined the majority and Justice O'Connor dissented. The City, suffering from decreasing population and economic distress, including an unemployment rate nearly double that of the State, sought to capitalize on the pharmaceutical company Pfizer's plans to build a $300 million research facility on a site adjacent to 90 acres in the City's Fort Trumbull area by adopting an economic revitalization plan for the adjacent property. At the City's request, a private nonprofit entity (NLDC) formulated an integrated economic development plan to transform the adjacent property into a "small urban village" with a waterfront conference hotel, shops and restaurants; commercial and recreational marinas; a pedestrian "riverwalk"; 80 new residences "organized into an urban neighborhood and linked by public walkway to the remainder of the development, including the [existing] state park"; a Coast Guard museum; research and development office space close to the Pfizer facility; and parking or retail services for visitors or in support of the marina, which was to be renovated. The State and the City approved the redevelopment plan, and the City authorized NLDC to implement it and to exercise the City's eminent domain power if necessary to acquire the property. Most of the property was acquired by negotiation but the owners of 15 properties—4 sought for office space and 11 for park or marina support—objected, claiming in a state court action that their properties, which were not alleged to be blighted or in poor condition, could not be taken for the purpose of private economic development without violating the "public use" requirement. A divided Connecticut Supreme Court rejected their claim, and the Supreme Court affirmed.

For the majority, Justice Stevens wrote in part:

"Two polar propositions are perfectly clear. On the one hand, it has long been accepted that the sovereign may not take the property of *A* for the sole purpose of transferring it to another private party *B*, even though *A* is paid just compensation. On the other hand, it is equally clear that a State may transfer property from one private party to another if future 'use by the public' is the purpose of the taking; the condemnation of land for a railroad with common-carrier duties is a familiar example. Neither of these propositions, however, determines the disposition of this case. As for the first proposition, the City would no doubt be forbidden from taking petitioners' land for the purpose of conferring a private benefit on a particular private party.... Nor would the City be allowed to take property under the mere pretext of a public purpose, when its actual purpose was to bestow a private benefit. The takings before us, however, would be executed pursuant to a 'carefully considered' development plan. 268 Conn., at 54 .... The trial judge and all the members of the Supreme Court of Connecticut agreed that there was no evidence of an illegitimate purpose in this case.[6] ...

"On the other hand, this is not a case in which the City is planning to open the condemned land—at least not in its entirety—to use by the general public. Nor will the private lessees of the land in any sense be required to operate like common carriers, making their services available to all comers. But although such a projected use would be sufficient to satisfy the public use requirement, this 'Court long ago rejected any literal requirement that condemned property be put into use for the general public.' . . . Not only was the 'use by the public' test difficult to administer (*e.g.,* what proportion of the public need have access to the property? at what price?) but it proved to be impractical given the diverse and always evolving needs of society. Accordingly, when this Court began applying the Fifth Amendment to the States at the close of the 19th century, it embraced the broader and more natural interpretation of public use as 'public purpose.' . . .

"The disposition of this case therefore turns on the question whether the City's development plan serves a 'public purpose.' Without exception, our cases have defined that concept broadly, reflecting our longstanding policy of deference to legislative judgments in this field.

" . . .

"Viewed as a whole, our jurisprudence has recognized that the needs of society have varied between different parts of the Nation, just as they have evolved over time in response to changed circumstances. Our earliest cases in particular embodied a strong theme of federalism, emphasizing the 'great respect' that we owe to state legislatures and state courts in discerning local public needs. . . . For more than a century, our public use jurisprudence has wisely eschewed rigid formulas and intrusive scrutiny in favor of affording legislatures broad latitude in determining what public needs justify the use of the takings power.

IV

"Those who govern the City were not confronted with the need to remove blight in the Fort Trumbull area, but their determination that the area was sufficiently distressed to justify a program of economic rejuvenation is entitled to our deference. The City has carefully formulated an economic development plan that it believes will provide appreciable benefits to the community, including—but by no means limited to—new jobs and increased tax revenue. As with other exercises in urban planning and development, the City is endeavoring to coordinate a variety of commercial, residential, and recreational uses of land, with the hope that they will form a whole greater than the sum of its parts. To effectuate this plan, the City has invoked a state statute that specifically authorizes the use of eminent domain to promote economic development. Given the comprehensive character of the plan, the thorough deliberation that preceded its adoption, and the limited scope of our review, it is

6. . . . And while the City intends to transfer certain of the parcels to a private developer in a long-term lease—which developer, in turn, is expected to lease the office space and so forth to other private tenants—the identities of those private parties were not known when the plan was adopted. It is, of course, difficult to accuse the government of having taken *A*'s property to benefit the private interests of *B* when the identity of *B* was unknown.

appropriate for us, as it was in *Berman*, to resolve the challenges of the individual owners, not on a piecemeal basis, but rather in light of the entire plan. Because that plan unquestionably serves a public purpose, the takings challenged here satisfy the public use requirement of the Fifth Amendment.

"To avoid this result, petitioners urge us to adopt a new bright-line rule that economic development does not qualify as a public use. Putting aside the unpersuasive suggestion that the City's plan will provide only purely economic benefits, neither precedent nor logic supports petitioners' proposal. Promoting economic development is a traditional and long accepted function of government. There is, moreover, no principled way of distinguishing economic development from the other public purposes that we have recognized. In our cases upholding takings that facilitated agriculture and mining, for example, we emphasized the importance of those industries to the welfare of the States in question . . . ; in *Berman*, we endorsed the purpose of transforming a blighted area into a 'well-balanced' community through redevelopment . . . ; in *Midkiff*, we upheld the interest in breaking up a land oligopoly that 'created artificial deterrents to the normal functioning of the State's residential land market,' . . . ; and in *Monsanto*, we accepted Congress' purpose of eliminating a 'significant barrier to entry in the pesticide market,'. . . . It would be incongruous to hold that the City's interest in the economic benefits to be derived from the development of the Fort Trumbull area has less of a public character than any of those other interests. Clearly, there is no basis for exempting economic development from our traditionally broad understanding of public purpose.

" . . . [T]he government's pursuit of a public purpose will often benefit individual private parties. . . .[16]

"It is further argued that without a bright-line rule nothing would stop a city from transferring citizen *A*'s property to citizen *B* for the sole reason that citizen *B* will put the property to a more productive use and thus pay more taxes. Such a one-to-one transfer of property, executed outside the confines of an integrated development plan, is not presented in this case. While such an unusual exercise of government power would certainly raise a suspicion that a private purpose was afoot, the hypothetical cases posited by petitioners can be confronted if and when they arise. They do not warrant the crafting of an artificial restriction on the concept of public use.

"Alternatively, petitioners maintain that for takings of this kind we should require a 'reasonable certainty' that the expected public benefits will actually accrue. Such a rule, however, would represent an even greater departure from our precedent. 'When the legislature's purpose is legitimate and its means are

16. Nor do our cases support Justice O'Connor's novel theory that the government may only take property and transfer it to private parties when the initial taking eliminates some 'harmful property use.' There was nothing 'harmful' about the nonblighted department store at issue in *Berman* . . . ; nothing 'harmful' about the lands at issue in the mining and agriculture cases . . . ; and certainly nothing 'harmful' about the trade secrets owned by the pesticide manufacturers in *Monsanto*. . . . In each case, the public purpose we upheld depended on a private party's *future* use of the concededly nonharmful property that was taken. By focusing on a property's future use, as opposed to its past use, our cases are faithful to the text of the Takings Clause. . . . Justice O'Connor's intimation that a 'public purpose' may not be achieved by the action of private parties confuses the *purpose* of a taking with its *mechanics*, a mistake we warned of in *Midkiff*. . . .

not irrational, our cases make clear that empirical debates over the wisdom of takings—no less than debates over the wisdom of other kinds of socioeconomic legislation—are not to be carried out in the federal courts.' *Midkiff*. . . . Indeed, earlier this Term we explained why similar practical concerns (among others) undermined the use of the 'substantially advances' formula in our regulatory takings doctrine. See *Lingle v. Chevron U.S.A. Inc.*, ... The disadvantages of a heightened form of review are especially pronounced in this type of case. Orderly implementation of a comprehensive redevelopment plan obviously requires that the legal rights of all interested parties be established before new construction can be commenced. A constitutional rule that required postponement of the judicial approval of every condemnation until the likelihood of success of the plan had been assured would unquestionably impose a significant impediment to the successful consummation of many such plans.

"Just as we decline to second-guess the City's considered judgments about the efficacy of its development plan, we also decline to second-guess the City's determinations as to what lands it needs to acquire in order to effectuate the project. . . .

". . . [N]othing in our opinion precludes any State from placing further restrictions on its exercise of the takings power. Indeed, many States already impose 'public use' requirements that are stricter than the federal baseline. . . . This Court's authority, however, extends only to determining whether the City's proposed condemnations are for a 'public use' within the meaning of the Fifth Amendment to the Federal Constitution. Because over a century of our case law interpreting that provision dictates an affirmative answer to that question, we may not grant petitioners the relief that they seek."

Justice Kennedy's concurring opinion emphasized the following:

"A court applying rational-basis review under the Public Use Clause should strike down a taking that, by a clear showing, is intended to favor a particular private party, with only incidental or pretextual public benefits, just as a court applying rational-basis review under the Equal Protection Clause must strike down a government classification that is clearly intended to injure a particular class of private parties, with only incidental or pretextual public justifications. See *Cleburne v. Cleburne Living Center, Inc.*, 473 U.S. 432, 446–447 (1985). . . .

"A court confronted with a plausible accusation of impermissible favoritism to private parties should treat the objection as a serious one and review the record to see if it has merit, though with the presumption that the government's actions were reasonable and intended to serve a public purpose. Here, the trial court conducted a careful and extensive inquiry. . . .

"The trial court concluded . . . that benefiting Pfizer was not 'the primary motivation or effect of this development plan'; instead, 'the primary motivation for [respondents] was to take advantage of Pfizer's presence.' . . . Likewise, the trial court concluded that '[t]here is nothing in the record to indicate that . . . [respondents] were motivated by a desire to aid [other] particular private entities.' . . . This case, then, survives the meaningful rational basis review that in my view is required under the Public Use Clause.

". . .

"My agreement with the Court that a presumption of invalidity is not warranted for economic development takings in general, or for the particular takings at issue in this case, does not foreclose the possibility that a more stringent standard of review than that announced in *Berman* and *Midkiff* might be appropriate for a more narrowly drawn category of takings. There may be private transfers in which the risk of undetected impermissible favoritism of private parties is so acute that a presumption (rebuttable or otherwise) of invalidity is warranted under the Public Use Clause.... This demanding level of scrutiny, however, is not required simply because the purpose of the taking is economic development.

"This is not the occasion for conjecture as to what sort of cases might justify a more demanding standard, but ... aspects of the instant case ... convince me no departure from *Berman* and *Midkiff* is appropriate here. This taking occurred in the context of a comprehensive development plan meant to address a serious city-wide depression, and the projected economic benefits of the project cannot be characterized as *de minimus*. The identity of most of the private beneficiaries were unknown at the time the city formulated its plans. The city complied with elaborate procedural requirements that facilitate review of the record and inquiry into the city's purposes. In sum, while there may be categories of cases in which the transfers are so suspicious, or the procedures employed so prone to abuse, or the purported benefits are so trivial or implausible, that courts should presume an impermissible private purpose, no such circumstances are present in this case."

Justice O'Connor's dissent, joined by Chief Justice Rehnquist and Justices Scalia and Thomas, objected that the Court's reasoning "that the incidental public benefits resulting from the subsequent ordinary use of private property render economic development takings 'for public use' wash[es] out any distinction between private and public use of property—and thereby effectively delete[s] the words 'for public use' from the Takings Clause of the Fifth Amendment." Her opinion reasoned in part:

"Where is the line between 'public' and 'private' property use? ... An external, judicial check on how the public use requirement is interpreted, however limited, is necessary if this constraint on government power is to retain any meaning....

"Our cases have generally identified three categories of takings that comply with the public use requirement.... First, the sovereign may transfer private property to public ownership—such as for a road, a hospital, or a military base.... Second, the sovereign may transfer private property to private parties, often common carriers, who make the property available for the public's use—such as with a railroad, a public utility, or a stadium.... But 'public ownership' and 'use-by-the-public' are sometimes too constricting and impractical ways to define the scope of the Public Use Clause. Thus we have allowed that, in certain circumstances and to meet certain exigencies, takings that serve a public purpose also satisfy the Constitution even if the property is destined for subsequent private use. See, *e.g., Berman v. Parker* ... ; *Hawaii Housing Authority v. Midkiff*....

"This case ... presents an issue of first impression: Are economic development takings constitutional? I would hold that they are not...."

" . . .

"[F]or all the emphasis on deference, *Berman* and *Midkiff* hewed to a bedrock principle without which our public use jurisprudence would collapse: 'A purely private taking could not withstand the scrutiny of the public use requirement; it would serve no legitimate purpose of government and would thus be void.' . . .

"The Court's holdings in *Berman* and *Midkiff* were true to the principle underlying the Public Use Clause. In both . . . the extraordinary, precondemnation use of the targeted property inflicted affirmative harm on society—in *Berman* through blight resulting from extreme poverty and in *Midkiff* through oligopoly resulting from extreme wealth. And in both cases, the relevant legislative body had found that eliminating the existing property use was necessary to remedy the harm. . . . Thus a public purpose was realized when the harmful use was eliminated. Because each taking *directly* achieved a public benefit, it did not matter that the property was turned over to private use. Here, in contrast, New London does not claim that [petitioners'] well-maintained homes are the source of any social harm. . . .

"In moving away from our decisions sanctioning the condemnation of harmful property use, the Court today significantly expands the meaning of public use. It holds that the sovereign may take private property currently put to ordinary private use, and give it over for new, ordinary private use, so long as the new use is predicted to generate some secondary benefit for the public—such as increased tax revenue, more jobs, maybe even aesthetic pleasure. But nearly any lawful use of real private property can be said to generate some incidental benefit to the public. Thus, if predicted (or even guaranteed) positive side-effects are enough to render transfer from one private party to another constitutional, then the words 'for public use' do not realistically exclude *any* takings, and thus do not exert any constraint on the eminent domain power.

" . . . The Court . . . suggests two limitations on what can be taken after today's decision. First, it maintains a role for courts in ferreting out takings whose sole purpose is to bestow a benefit on the private transferee—without detailing how courts are to conduct that complicated inquiry. For his part, Justice Kennedy suggests that courts may divine illicit purpose by a careful review of the record and the process by which a legislature arrived at the decision to take—without specifying what courts should look for in a case with different facts, how they will know if they have found it, and what to do if they do not. . . . The trouble with economic development takings is that private benefit and incidental public benefit are, by definition, merged and mutually reinforcing. In this case, for example, any boon for Pfizer or the plan's developer is difficult to disaggregate from the promised public gains in taxes and jobs.

"Even if there were a practical way to isolate the motives behind a given taking, the gesture toward a purpose test is theoretically flawed. If it is true that incidental public benefits from new private use are enough to ensure the 'public purpose' in a taking, why should it matter, as far as the Fifth Amendment is concerned, what inspired the taking in the first place? How much the government does or does not desire to benefit a favored private party has no bearing on whether an economic development taking will or will not generate secondary benefit for the public. And whatever the reason for a given condemnation, the effect is the same from the constitutional perspective—private property is forcibly relinquished to new private ownership.

"A second proposed limitation is implicit in the Court's opinion[—]that eminent domain may only be used to upgrade—not downgrade—property. At best this makes the Public Use Clause redundant with the Due Process Clause, which already prohibits irrational government action.... The Court rightfully admits, however, that the judiciary cannot get bogged down in predictive judgments about whether the public will actually be better off after a property transfer. In any event, this constraint has no realistic import. For who among us can say she already makes the most productive or attractive possible use of her property? The specter of condemnation hangs over all property. Nothing is to prevent the State from replacing any Motel 6 with a Ritz-Carlton, any home with a shopping mall, or any farm with a factory....

"The Court also puts special emphasis on facts peculiar to this case.... But none has legal significance to blunt the force of today's holding. If legislative prognostications about the secondary public benefits of a new use can legitimate a taking, there is nothing in the Court's rule or in Justice Kennedy's gloss on that rule to prohibit property transfers generated with less care, that are less comprehensive, that happen to result from less elaborate process, whose only projected advantage is the incidence of higher taxes, or that hope to transform an already prosperous city into an even more prosperous one.

"...

"Any property may now be taken for the benefit of another private party, but the fallout from this decision will not be random. The beneficiaries are likely to be those citizens with disproportionate influence and power in the political process, including large corporations and development firms. As for the victims, the government now has license to transfer property from those with fewer resources to those with more. The Founders cannot have intended this perverse result.... "

A separate dissent by Justice Thomas urged a return to what he perceived to be the "original meaning of the Public Use Clause: that the government may take property only if it actually uses or gives the public a legal right to use the property"—and not when "the purpose of the taking is legitimately public." In his view, the text of the Fifth Amendment, the early history of eminent domain practice, and the alleged mistake in conflating the public use requirement of the takings clause with the public purpose requirement of the due process clause, all point in the direction of reconsidering the error of "*Berman* and *Midkiff* [in] equating the eminent domain power with the police power of States." He contended that "[t]he 'public purpose' test applied by *Berman* and *Midkiff* ... cannot be applied in a principled manner" and that "[i]t is far easier to analyze whether the government owns or the public has a legal right to use the taken property than to ask whether the taking has a 'purely private purpose'—unless the Court means to eliminate public use scrutiny of takings entirely." Finally, he argued that "extending the concept of public purpose to encompass any economically beneficial goal guarantees that these losses will fall disproportionately on poor communities. Those communities are not only systematically less likely to put their lands to the highest and best social use, but are also the least politically powerful. If ever there were justification for intrusive judicial review of constitutional provisions that protect 'discrete and insular minorities,' *United States v. Carolene Products Co.* ..., surely that principle would apply with great force to the powerless groups and individuals the Public Use Clause protects."

1. RESTRICTIONS ON PROPERTY USE

Page 568. Add at end of subsection:

LINGLE v. CHEVRON U. S. A. INC., 125 S.Ct. 2074 (2005). Although the *Lucas* and *Tahoe-Sierra* cases both involve claims that government denial of economically viable use of property constitutes a taking, they each incidentally refer to the separate doctrinal formulation initially set forth in Agins v. City of Tiburon, 447 U.S. 255, 100 S.Ct. 2138, 65 L.Ed.2d 106 (1980), that government regulation of private property "effects a taking if [such regulation] does not substantially advance legitimate state interests.... " Applying that independent rule, the lower federal courts in *Lingle* held that Act 257, a Hawaii statute designed to control retail gasoline prices by limiting the rent oil companies could charge dealers leasing service stations from them, effected "an unconstitutional regulatory taking." Because existing lessee-dealers could transfer occupancy rights to a new lessee and charge a premium reflecting the rent reduction, and because in any event the oil company lessors could unilaterally raise wholesale fuel prices in order to offset the reduction in their rental income, the lower courts ruled, there would be no savings to pass on to consumers of gasoline, and, hence, the statute failed to substantially advance a legitimate state interest.

A unanimous Supreme Court reversed, "correct[ing] course" by holding that the *Agins* " 'substantially advances' formula is not a valid takings test, and indeed ... has no proper place in our takings jurisprudence." Justice O'Connor's opinion for the Court noted that "in no case have we found a compensable taking based on such an inquiry" and reasoned in significant part as follows:

"Although our regulatory takings jurisprudence cannot be characterized as unified, the[] three inquiries reflected in ... *Loretto, Lucas*, and *Penn Central* ... share a common touchstone. Each aims to identify regulatory actions that are functionally equivalent to the classic taking in which government directly appropriates private property or ousts the owner from his domain. Accordingly, each ... focuses directly upon the severity of the burden that government imposes upon private property rights. [P]hysical takings require compensation because of the unique burden they impose: A permanent physical invasion, however minimal the economic cost it entails, eviscerates the owner's right to exclude others from entering and using her property—perhaps the most fundamental of all property interests.... In the *Lucas* context, ... the complete elimination of a property's value is the determinative factor.... And the *Penn Central* inquiry turns in large part, albeit not exclusively, upon the magnitude of a regulation's economic impact and the degree to which it interferes with legitimate property interests.

"... Although a number of our takings precedents have recited the 'substantially advances' formula minted in *Agins*, this is our first opportunity to consider its validity as a freestanding takings test. We conclude that this formula prescribes an inquiry in the nature of a due process, not a takings, test, and that it has no proper place in our takings jurisprudence.

"There is no question that the 'substantially advances' formula was derived from due process, not takings, precedents....

" ... [W]hen *Agins* was decided, there had been some history of referring to deprivations of property without due process of law as 'takings,' ... and the Court had yet to clarify whether 'regulatory takings' claims were properly cognizable under the Takings Clause or the Due Process Clause ....

"Although *Agins'* reliance on due process precedents is understandable, the language the Court selected was regrettably imprecise. The 'substantially advances' formula suggests a means-ends test: It asks, in essence, whether a regulation of private property is *effective* in achieving some legitimate public purpose. An inquiry of this nature has some logic in the context of a due process challenge, for a regulation that fails to serve any legitimate governmental objective may be so arbitrary or irrational that it runs afoul of the Due Process Clause.... But such a test is not a valid method of discerning whether private property has been 'taken' for purposes of the Fifth Amendment.

"In stark contrast to the three regulatory takings tests discussed above, the 'substantially advances' inquiry reveals nothing about the *magnitude or character of the burden* a particular regulation imposes upon private property rights. Nor does it provide any information about how any regulatory burden is *distributed* among property owners. In consequence, this test does not help to identify those regulations whose effects are functionally comparable to government appropriation or invasion of private property; it is tethered neither to the text of the Takings Clause nor to the basic justification for allowing regulatory actions to be challenged under the Clause.

" ... A test that tells us nothing about the actual burden imposed on property rights, or how that burden is allocated[,] cannot tell us when justice might require that the burden be spread among taxpayers through the payment of compensation. The owner of a property subject to a regulation that *effectively* serves a legitimate state interest may be just as singled out and just as burdened as the owner of a property subject to an *ineffective* regulation. It would make little sense to say that the second owner has suffered a taking while the first has not. Likewise, an ineffective regulation may not significantly burden property rights at all, and it may distribute any burden broadly and evenly among property owners. The notion that such a regulation nevertheless 'takes' private property for public use merely by virtue of its ineffectiveness or foolishness is untenable.

"... [T]he 'substantially advances' inquiry probes the regulation's underlying validity. But such an inquiry is logically prior to and distinct from the question whether a regulation effects a taking, for the Takings Clause presupposes that the government has acted in pursuit of a valid public purpose....

"... Chevron has not clearly argued—let alone established—that it has been singled out to bear any particularly severe regulatory burden. Rather, the gravamen of Chevron's claim is simply that Hawaii's rent cap will not actually serve the State's legitimate interest in protecting consumers against high gasoline prices. Whatever the merits of that claim, it does not sound under the Takings Clause. Chevron plainly does not seek compensation for a taking of its property for a legitimate public use, but rather an injunction against the enforcement of a regulation that it alleges to be fundamentally arbitrary and irrational.

" ... The *Agins* formula can be read to demand heightened means-ends review of virtually any regulation of private property. If so interpreted, it would require courts to scrutinize the efficacy of a vast array of state and federal regulations—a task for which courts are not well suited. Moreover, it would empower—and might often require—courts to substitute their predictive judgments for those of elected legislatures and expert agencies.

" ... To resolve Chevron's takings claim, the District Court was required to choose between the views of two opposing economists as to whether Hawaii's rent control statute would help to prevent concentration and supracompetitive prices in the State's retail gasoline market. Finding one expert to be 'more persuasive' than the other, the court concluded that the Hawaii Legislature's chosen regulatory strategy would not actually achieve its objectives.... Along the way, the court determined that the State was not entitled to enact a prophylactic rent cap without actual evidence that oil companies had charged, or would charge, excessive rents.... We find the proceedings below remarkable, to say the least, given that we have long eschewed such heightened scrutiny when addressing substantive due process challenges to government regulation.... The reasons for deference to legislative judgments about the need for, and likely effectiveness of, regulatory actions are by now well established, and we think they are no less applicable here."

2. MANDATED ACCESS TO PROPERTY

Page 579. Add at end of subsection:

LINGLE v. CHEVRON U. S. A. INC., 125 S.Ct. 2074 (2005). As noted, supra, p. 26, the Court in *Lingle* unanimously repudiated the view it had expressed in Agins v. City of Tiburon, 447 U.S. 255, 100 S.Ct. 2138, 65 L.Ed.2d 106 (1980), and many subsequent cases, that government regulation of private property "effects a taking if [such regulation] does not substantially advance legitimate state interests.... " Part III of Justice O'Connor's opinion "emphasize[d] that our holding today—that the 'substantially advances' formula is not a valid takings test—does not require us to disturb any of our prior holdings." It continued:

"It might be argued that this formula played a role in our decisions in *Nollan v. California Coastal Comm'n*, 483 U.S. 825 (1987), and *Dolan v. City of Tigard*, 512 U.S. 374 (1994).... But while the Court drew upon the language of *Agins* in these cases, it did not apply the 'substantially advances' test that is the subject of today's decision. Both *Nollan* and *Dolan* involved Fifth Amendment takings challenges to adjudicative land-use exactions—specifically, government demands that a landowner dedicate an easement allowing public access to her property as a condition of obtaining a development permit....

"In each case, the Court began with the premise that, had the government simply appropriated the easement in question, this would have been a *per se* physical taking.... The question was whether the government could, without paying the compensation that would otherwise be required upon effecting such a taking, demand the easement as a condition for granting a development permit the government was entitled to deny. The Court in *Nollan* answered in the affirmative, provided that the exaction would substantially advance the same government interest that would furnish a valid ground for denial of the permit.... The Court further refined this requirement in *Dolan,* holding that an adjudicative exaction requiring dedication of private property must also be 'rough[ly] proportiona[l]' ... both in nature and extent to the impact of the proposed development."...

"Although *Nollan* and *Dolan* quoted *Agins'* language, ... the rule those decisions established is entirely distinct from the 'substantially advances' test we address today. Whereas the 'substantially advances' inquiry before us now is unconcerned with the degree or type of burden a regulation places upon property, *Nollan* and *Dolan* both involved dedications of property so onerous that, outside the exactions context, they would be deemed *per se* physical takings. In neither case did the Court question whether the exaction would substantially advance *some* legitimate state interest.... Rather, the issue was whether the exactions substantially advanced the *same* interests that land-use authorities asserted would allow them to deny the permit altogether. As the Court explained in *Dolan*, these cases involve a special application of the 'doctrine of "unconstitutional conditions,"' which provides that 'the government may not require a person to give up a constitutional right—here the right to receive just compensation when property is taken for a public use—in exchange for a discretionary benefit conferred by the government where the benefit has little or no relationship to the property.' ... That is worlds apart from a rule that says a regulation affecting property constitutes a taking on its face solely because it does not substantially advance a legitimate government interest. In short, *Nollan* and *Dolan* cannot be characterized as applying the 'substantially advances' test we address today, and our decision should not be read to disturb these precedents."

CHAPTER 10

The Equal Protection Clause and the Review of the Reasonableness of Legislation

SECTION 3. Suspect Classifications

B. Racial Segregation in Schools and Other Public Facilities

Page 731. Add at end of Note, "Segregation in Public Facilities Other than Schools":

More than four decades later, in Johnson v. California, ___ U.S. ___, 125 S.Ct. 1141, 160 L.Ed.2d 949 (2005), a divided Court insisted that strict scrutiny be applied to an unwritten California policy segregating prisoners in double cells (but not the prison generally) for up to 60 days after they arrive at a new prison, despite the claims of corrections officials that the temporary segregation was necessary during a period of inmate evaluation to prevent violence associated with racial gangs. With Chief Justice Rehnquist not participating, Justice O'Connor's majority opinion reasoned in part that "by insisting that inmates be housed only with other inmates of the same race, it is possible that prison officials will breed further hostility among prisoners and reinforce racial and ethnic divisions. By perpetuating the notion that race matters most, racial segregation of inmates 'may exacerbate the very patterns of [violence that it is] said to counteract.' " She "decline[d] the invitation" to make an exception for the prison context, where for certain fundamental constitutional rights the Court in Turner v. Safley, 482 U.S. 78, 89, 107 S.Ct. 2254, 96 L.Ed.2d 64 (1987), has required only that a burdensome regulation be "reasonably related" to "legitimate penological interests." Unlike the constitutional rights to which the deferential standard of *Turner* properly applied, "[t]he right not to be discriminated against based on one's race is ... not a right that need necessarily be compromised for the sake of proper prison administration. On the contrary, compliance with the Fourteenth Amendment's ban on racial discrimination ... bolsters the legitimacy of the entire criminal justice system." The majority was convinced that "[i]n the prison context, when the government's power is at its apex, ... searching judicial review of racial classifications is necessary to guard against invidious discrimination"; that "[t]he 'necessities of prison security and discipline' ... are a compelling government interest justifying only those uses of race that are narrowly tailored to address those necessities"; and that on remand, although "[s]trict scrutiny does not preclude the ability of prison officials to address the compelling interest in prison safety[, p]rison administrators . . . will have to demonstrate that any race-based policies are narrowly tailored to that end.''

A dissent by Justice Stevens concluded that the record as it stood showed the policy was unconstitutional, for it was ''based on a conclusive presumption that housing inmates of different races together creates an unacceptable risk of racial violence''; ''scant empirical evidence'' supported that presumption; and a ''very real risk that prejudice (whether conscious or not) partly underlies the . . . policy'' undermined it. A polar opposite dissent by Justice Thomas, joined by Justice Scalia, emphasized ''how limited the policy . . . is'' of racial segregation of ''a portion of [California's] inmates, in a part of its prisons, for brief periods . . . until the State can arrange permanent housing'' and argued that the Court should apply *Turner* and defer to the expert judgment of prison officials. Those officials had asserted that ''housing inmates in double cells without regard to race threatens not only prison discipline, but also the physical safety of inmates and staff . . . because double cells are especially dangerous. The risk of racial violence in public areas of prisons is high, and the tightly confined, private conditions of cells hazard even more violence.'' Furthermore, ''Johnson has never argued that California's policy is motivated by anything other than a desire to protect inmates and staff.'' In any event, ''the Constitution's usual demands . . . have always been lessened inside . . . prison walls'' and the majority's ''second-guessing'' fell ''far short of the compelling showing needed to overcome the deference we owe to prison administrators.''

SECTION 4. PROTECTION OF PERSONAL LIBERTIES

D. COURT ACCESS, WELFARE, AND THE POOR

Page 1057. Add at end of Note, ''The Rights of the Poor Defendant in the Criminal Justice System'':

The Due Process and Equal Protection Clauses were held to require the appointment of counsel, however, in connection with preparing an application for discretionary leave to seek a first-tier appeal from a challenged conviction based on a guilty plea or a plea of nolo contendere. Halbert v. Michigan, 125 S.Ct. 2582 (2005). Justice Ginsburg's majority opinion reasoned that a discretionary first appeal should be treated the same as a first appeal as of right under Douglas v. California, rather than as a discretionary subsequent appeal under Ross v. Moffitt, largely because of two features of Michigan's appellate process following plea-based convictions: ''First, in determining how to dispose of an application for leave to appeal, Michigan's intermediate appellate court looks to the merits of the claims made in the application. Second, indigent defendants pursuing first-tier review in the Court of Appeals are generally ill equipped to represent themselves.'' Unlike discretionary review following a first appeal as of right, as in *Ross*, when the first appeal is discretionary a ''first-tier review applicant, forced to act *pro se,* will face a record unreviewed by appellate counsel, and will be equipped with no attorney's brief prepared for, or reasoned opinion by, a court of review[,]'' rendering ''a *pro se* applicant's entitlement to seek leave to appeal . . . more formal than real.'' Justice Ginsburg also noted the low rates of inmate literacy and reasoned that "[n]avigating the appellate process without a lawyer's assistance is a perilous endeavor for a layperson, and well beyond the competence of individuals, like Halbert, who have little education, learning disabilities, and mental impairments."

Justice Thomas, joined by Justice Scalia and Chief Justice Rehnquist, dissented, finding the Court's decision "an unwarranted extension of" *Douglas*.

CHAPTER 11

DEFINING THE SCOPE OF "LIBERTY" AND "PROPERTY" PROTECTED BY THE DUE PROCESS CLAUSE—THE PROCEDURAL DUE PROCESS CASES

SECTION 1. WHEN DOES DUE PROCESS MANDATE CONSTITUTIONAL PROCEDURES?

A. WHAT "PROPERTY" AND "LIBERTY" IS PROTECTED?

Page 1103. Add after American Manufacturers Mutual Insurance Co. v. Sullivan:

TOWN OF CASTLE ROCK v. GONZALES, 125 S.Ct. 2796 (2005). In violation of a restraining order issued in conjunction with divorce proceedings, and without notice, an estranged father took his three daughters from the front of the family home. Tragically, several hours later he murdered them and thereafter was killed in a shoot-out with police. The mother sued the Town, alleging that her repeated, unsuccessful efforts throughout the night to have the police enforce the restraining order were thwarted by a police department policy or custom of failing to respond properly and tolerating non-enforcement of restraining orders, thereby depriving her, without due process, of a statutorily-based property interest in police enforcement of the restraining order.

The Court held that she "did not, for purposes of the Due Process Clause, have a property interest in police enforcement of the restraining order against her husband." Noting that "a benefit is not a protected entitlement if government officials may grant or deny it in their discretion[,]" Justice Scalia's opinion wrote that "the central state-law question is whether Colorado law gave respondent a right to police enforcement of the restraining order"—a question as to which the Court found deference to the Tenth Circuit Court of Appeals "inappropriate," primarily because its opinion "did not draw upon a deep well of state-specific expertise, but consisted primarily of quoting language from the restraining order, the statutory text, and a state-legislative-hearing transcript." The Court's own examination led it to conclude that Colorado statutory provisions apparently obligating police to use "every reasonable means to enforce a restraining order," and to "arrest, or if an arrest would be impractical under the circumstances, seek a warrant for the arrest of a restrained person" when there is probable cause that the person has violated the order, did not "truly ma[k]e enforcement of restraining orders *mandatory*. A well established tradition of police discretion has long coexisted with apparently mandatory arrest statutes." Accordingly, "a true mandate of police action would require some stronger indication from the Colorado Legislature . . . ."

Justice Scalia also wrote:

"Respondent does not specify the precise means of enforcement that the Colorado restraining-order statute assertedly mandated—whether her interest lay in having police arrest her husband, having them seek a warrant for his arrest, or having them 'use every reasonable means, up to and including arrest, to enforce the order's terms . . . ' Such indeterminacy is not the hallmark of a duty that is mandatory. Nor can someone be safely deemed 'entitled' to something when the identity of the alleged entitlement is vague. . . . The dissent ultimately contends that the obligations under the statute were quite precise: either make an arrest or (if that is impractical) seek an arrest warrant. The problem with this is that the seeking of an arrest warrant would be an entitlement to nothing but procedure—which . . . can[not] be the basis for a property interest. . . . After the warrant is sought, it remains within the discretion of a judge whether to grant it, and after it is granted, it remains within the discretion of the police whether and when to execute it. Respondent would have been assured nothing but the seeking of a warrant. This is not the sort of 'entitlement' out of which a property interest is created.

"Even if the statute could be said to have made enforcement of restraining orders 'mandatory' because of the domestic-violence context of the underlying statute, that would not necessarily mean that state law gave *respondent* an entitlement to *enforcement* of the mandate. Making the actions of government employees obligatory can serve various legitimate ends other than the conferral of a benefit on a specific class of people. . . .

"Respondent's alleged interest stems only from a State's *statutory* scheme—from a restraining order that was authorized by and tracked precisely the statute on which the Court of Appeals relied. She does not assert that she has any common-law or contractual entitlement to enforcement. If she was given a statutory entitlement, we would expect to see some indication of that in the statute itself. Although Colorado's statute spoke of 'protected person[s]' such as respondent, it did so in connection with matters other than a right to enforcement. . . . Perhaps most importantly, the statute spoke directly to the protected person's power to 'initiate contempt proceedings against the restrained person if the order [was] issued in a civil action or request the prosecuting attorney to initiate contempt proceedings if the order [was] issued in a criminal action.' . . . The protected person's express power to 'initiate' civil contempt proceedings contrasts tellingly with the mere ability to 'request' initiation of criminal contempt proceedings—and even more dramatically with the complete silence about any power to 'request' (much less demand) that an arrest be made.

" . . .

"Even if we were to think otherwise concerning the creation of an entitlement by Colorado, it is by no means clear that an individual entitlement to enforcement of a restraining order could constitute a 'property' interest for purposes of the Due Process Clause. Such a right would not, of course, resemble any traditional conception of property. Although that alone does not disqualify it from due process protection, as *Roth* and its progeny show, the right to have a restraining order enforced does not 'have some ascertainable monetary value,' as even our '*Roth*-type property-as-entitlement' cases have implicitly required.... Perhaps most radically, the alleged property interest here arises *incidentally*, not out of some new species of government benefit or service, but out of a function that government actors have always performed—to wit, arresting people who they have probable cause to believe have committed a criminal offense.

" ... In this case ... '[t]he simple distinction between government action that directly affects a citizen's legal rights ... and action that is directed against a third party and affects the citizen only indirectly or incidentally, provides a sufficient answer to' respondent's reliance on cases that found government-provided services to be entitlements."

Justice Souter's concurring opinion, joined by Justice Breyer, said in part:

"[Gonzales'] argument is unconventional because the state-law benefit for which it claims federal procedural protection is itself a variety of procedural regulation, a set of rules to be followed by officers exercising the State's executive power: use all reasonable means to enforce, arrest upon demonstrable probable cause, get a warrant, and so on.

"When her argument is [so] understood ... , a further reason appears for rejecting its call to apply *Roth,* a reason that would apply even if the statutory mandates to the police were absolute, leaving the police with no discretion when the beneficiary of a protective order insists upon its enforcement.... [The] argument is at odds with the rule that '[p]rocess is not an end in itself. Its constitutional purpose is to protect a substantive interest to which the individual has a legitimate claim of entitlement.' ... Just as a State cannot diminish a property right, once conferred, by attaching less than generous procedure to its deprivation, ... neither does a State create a property right merely by ordaining beneficial procedure unconnected to some articulable substantive guarantee.... [W]e have not identified property with procedure as such. State rules of executive procedure, however important, may be nothing more than rules of executive procedure.

"Thus, in every instance of property recognized by this Court as calling for federal procedural protection, the property has been distinguishable from the procedural obligations imposed on state officials to protect it. Whether welfare benefits, *Goldberg v. Kelly*, 397 U.S. 254 (1970), attendance at public schools, *Goss v. Lopez*, 419 U.S. 565 (1975), utility services, *Memphis Light, Gas & Water Div. v. Craft*, 436 U.S. 1 (1978), public employment, *Perry v. Sindermann*, 408 U.S. 593 (1972), professional licenses, *Barry v. Barchi*, 443 U.S. 55 (1979), and so on, the property interest recognized in our cases has always existed apart from state procedural protection before the Court has recognized a constitutional claim to protection by federal process.... There is no articulable distinction between the object of Gonzales's asserted entitlement and the process she desires in order to protect her entitlement; both amount to certain steps to be taken by the police to protect her family and herself. Gonzales's claim would thus take us beyond *Roth* or any other recognized theory of Fourteenth Amendment due process, by collapsing the distinction between property protected and the process that protects it, and would federalize every mandatory state-law direction to executive officers whose performance on the job can be vitally significant to individuals affected.

"The procedural directions involved here ... presuppose no enforceable substantive entitlement, and *Roth* does not raise them to federally enforceable status in the name of due process."

Justice Stevens dissented, joined by Justice Ginsburg. Among the points he emphasized were that the States had passed a wave of "mandatory arrest" statutes in the domestic violence context in the 1980s and 1990s "with the unmistakable goal of eliminating police discretion in this area"; that "the Colorado statute at issue in this case was enacted for the benefit of the narrow class of persons who are beneficiaries of domestic restraining orders, and ... the order at issue in this case was specifically intended to provide protection to respondent and her children"; and "that a citizen's interest in the government's commitment to provide police enforcement in certain defined circumstances ... is just as concrete and worthy of protection as her interest in any other important service the government or a private firm has undertaken to provide." In his view, "under the statute, the police were *required* to provide enforcement; *they lacked the discretion to do nothing*.... Under the statute, if the police have probable cause that a violation has occurred, enforcement consists of either making an immediate arrest or seeking a warrant and then executing an arrest—traditional, well-defined tasks that law enforcement officers perform every day." Moreover, "[b]ecause the statute's guarantee of police enforcement is triggered by, and operates only in reference to, a judge's granting of a restraining order in favor of an identified " 'protected person,' " there is simply no room to suggest that such a person has received merely an " 'incidental' " or " 'indirect' " benefit." In the concluding section of his dissent, Justice Stevens wrote in part:

"Given that Colorado law has quite clearly eliminated the police's discretion to deny enforcement, respondent is correct that she had much more than a 'unilateral expectation' that the restraining order would be enforced; rather, she had a 'legitimate claim of entitlement' to enforcement. *Roth* ....

"Police enforcement of a restraining order is a government service that is no less concrete and no less valuable than other government services, such as education. The relative novelty of recognizing this type of property interest is explained by the relative novelty of the domestic violence statutes creating a mandatory arrest duty; before this innovation, the unfettered discretion that characterized police enforcement defeated any citizen's 'legitimate claim of entitlement' to this service.... Colorado law *guaranteed* the provision of a certain service, in certain defined circumstances, to a certain class of beneficiaries, and respondent reasonably relied on that guarantee. As we observed in *Roth*, '[i]t is a purpose of the ancient institution of property to protect those claims upon which people rely in their daily lives, reliance that must not be arbitrarily undermined.' ... Surely, if respondent had contracted with a private security firm to provide her and her daughters with protection from her husband, it would be apparent that she possessed a property interest in such a contract. Here, Colorado undertook a comparable obligation, and respondent—with restraining order in hand—justifiably relied on that undertaking. Respondent's claim of entitlement to this promised service is no less legitimate than the other claims our cases have upheld, and no less concrete than a hypothetical agreement with a private firm. The fact that it is based on a statutory enactment and a judicial order entered for her special protection, rather than on a formal contract, does not provide a principled basis for refusing to consider it 'property' worthy of constitutional protection.[20]"

Page 1114. Add after Sandin v. Conner:

WILKINSON V. AUSTIN, 125 S.Ct. 2384 (2005). Prisoners challenged the procedures Ohio adopted for assignment to the Ohio State Penitentiary (OSP)—its most restrictive, highest security prison, designed to segregate the most dangerous prisoners from the general prison population. The Court unanimously held that under *Sandin* the inmates possessed a liberty interest in avoiding assignment to OSP but that Ohio's informal, nonadversary procedures were adequate to satisfy due process under Mathews v. Eldridge, 424 U.S. 319, 96 S.Ct. 893, 47 L.Ed.2d 18 (1976), discussed infra, p. 1120. With respect to the existence of a cognizable liberty interest, the Court noted but did not resolve a divergence among the Courts of Appeals about the application of *Sandin*'s criterion of whether a freedom from restraint "imposes atypical and significant hardship on the inmate in relation to the ordinary incidents of prison life" stemming from the difficulty of "identifying the baseline from which to measure what is atypical and significant in any prison system." Instead, the Court said:

"... [W]e are satisfied that assignment to OSP imposes an atypical and significant hardship under any plausible baseline.

"For an inmate placed in OSP, almost all human contact is prohibited, even to the point that conversation is not permitted cell to cell; the light, though it may be dimmed, is on for 24 hours; exercise is for 1 hour per day, but only in a small indoor room. Save perhaps for the especially severe limitations on all human contact, these conditions likely would apply to most solitary confinement facilities, but here there are two added components. First is the duration. Unlike the 30-day placement in *Sandin*, placement at OSP is indefinite and, after an initial 30-day review, is reviewed just annually. Second is that placement disqualifies an otherwise eligible inmate for parole consideration.... While any of these conditions standing alone might not be sufficient to create a liberty interest, taken together they impose an atypical and significant hardship within the correctional context. It follows that respondents have a liberty interest in avoiding assignment to OSP....

"OSP's harsh conditions may well be necessary and appropriate in light of the danger that high-risk inmates pose both to prison officials and to other prisoners. That necessity, however, does not diminish our conclusion that the conditions give rise to a liberty interest in their avoidance."

20. ... Justice Souter ... misunderstands respondent's claim.... [R]espondent is in fact asserting a substantive interest in the 'enforcement of the restraining order.'[—] a tangible, substantive act. If an estranged husband violates a restraining order by abducting children, and the police succeed in enforcing the order, the person holding the restraining order has undeniably just received a substantive benefit. As in other procedural due process cases, respondent is arguing that the police officers failed to follow fair procedures in ascertaining whether the statutory criteria that trigger their obligation to provide enforcement—*i.e.*, an outstanding order plus probable cause that it is being violated—were satisfied in her case.... It is Justice Souter, not respondent, who makes the mistake of 'collapsing the distinction between property protected and the process that protects it.'

...

PART IV

Constitutional Protection of Expression and Conscience

CHAPTER 15

Protection of Penumbral First Amendment Rights

SECTION 3. Freedom of Association

D. Compulsory Association Membership

Page 1599. Replace Board of Regents of University of Wisconsin System v. Southworth:

Johanns v. Livestock Marketing Association

___ U.S. ___, 125 S.Ct. 2055, ___ L.Ed.2d ___ (2005).

Justice Scalia delivered the opinion of the Court.

For the third time in eight years, we consider whether a federal program that finances generic advertising to promote an agricultural product violates the First Amendment. In these cases, unlike the previous two, the dispositive question is whether the generic advertising at issue is the Government's own speech and therefore is exempt from First Amendment scrutiny.

I

A

The Beef Promotion and Research Act of 1985 (Beef Act or Act) ... announces a federal policy of promoting the marketing and consumption of "beef and beef products," using funds raised by an assessment on cattle sales and importation.... The statute directs the Secretary of Agriculture to implement this policy by issuing a Beef Promotion and Research Order (Beef Order or Order) ... and specifies four key terms it must contain: The Secretary is to appoint a Cattlemen's Beef Promotion and Research Board (Beef Board or Board), whose members are to be a geographically representative group of beef producers and importers, nominated by trade associations.... The Beef Board is to convene an Operating Committee, composed of 10 Beef Board members and 10 representatives named by a federation of state beef councils ... The Secretary is to impose a $1-per-head assessment (or "checkoff") on all sales or importation of cattle and a comparable assessment on imported beef products.... And the assessment is to be used to fund beef-related projects, including promotional campaigns, designed by the Operating Committee and approved by the Secretary....

. . .

B

Respondents are two associations whose members collect and pay the checkoff, and several individuals who raise and sell cattle subject to the checkoff.... They sued the Secretary, the Department of Agriculture, and the Board in Federal District Court on a number of constitutional and statutory grounds not before us—in particular, that the Board impermissibly used checkoff funds to send communications supportive of the beef program to beef producers....

While the litigation was pending, we held in United States v. United Foods, Inc., ... that a mandatory checkoff for generic mushroom advertising violated the First Amendment. Noting that the mushroom program closely resembles the beef program, respondents amended their complaint to assert a First Amendment challenge to the use of the beef checkoff for promotional activity....

After a bench trial, the District Court ruled for respondents on their First Amendment claim....

The Court of Appeals for the Eighth Circuit affirmed....

. . .

II

We have sustained First Amendment challenges to allegedly compelled expression in two categories of cases: true "compelled speech" cases, in which an individual is obliged personally to express a message he disagrees with, imposed by the government; and "compelled subsidy" cases, in which an individual is required by the government to subsidize a message he disagrees with, expressed by a private entity. We have not heretofore considered the First Amendment consequences of government-compelled subsidy of the government's own speech.

We first invalidated an outright compulsion of speech in West Virginia Bd. of Ed. v. Barnette, 319 U.S. 624 (1943). . . . We held that the First Amendment does not "le[ave] it open to public authorities to compel [a person] to utter" a message with which he does not agree. . . . Likewise, in Wooley v. Maynard, 430 U.S. 705 (1977), we held that requiring a New Hampshire couple to bear the State's motto, "Live Free or Die," on their cars' license plates was an impermissible compulsion of expression. Obliging people to "use their private property as a 'mobile billboard' for the State's ideological message" amounted to impermissible compelled expression. . . .

The reasoning of these compelled-speech cases has been carried over to certain instances in which individuals are compelled not to speak, but to subsidize a private message with which they disagree. Thus, although we have upheld state-imposed requirements that lawyers be members of the state bar and pay its annual dues, and that public-school teachers either join the labor union representing their "shop" or pay "service fees" equal to the union dues, we have invalidated the use of the compulsory fees to fund speech on political matters. See Keller v. State Bar of Cal., 496 U.S. 1, (1990); Abood v. Detroit Bd. of Ed., 431 U.S. 209 (1977). Bar or union speech with such content, we held, was not germane to the regulatory interests that justified compelled membership, and accordingly, making those who disagreed with it pay for it violated the First Amendment. . . .

These latter cases led us to sustain a compelled-subsidy challenge to an assessment very similar to the beef checkoff, imposed to fund mushroom advertising. *United Foods*, supra. . . . Deciding the case on the assumption that the advertising was private speech, not government speech, . . . we concluded that *Abood* and *Keller* were controlling. . . .

III

Respondents . . . assert that the challenged promotional campaigns differ dispositively from the type of government speech that, our cases suggest, is not susceptible to First Amendment challenge. They point to the role of the Beef Board and its Operating Committee in designing the promotional campaigns, and to the use of a mandatory assessment on beef producers to fund the advertising. We consider each in turn.

A

The Secretary of Agriculture does not write ad copy himself. Rather, the Beef Board's promotional campaigns are designed by the Beef Board's Operating Committee, only half of whose members are Beef Board members appointed by the Secretary. . . . Respondents contend that speech whose content is effectively controlled by a nongovernmental entity—the Operating Committee—cannot be considered "government speech." We need not address this contention, because we reject its premise. The message of the promotional campaigns is effectively controlled by the Federal Government itself.

. . .

B

Respondents also contend that the beef program does not qualify as "government speech" because it is funded by a targeted assessment on beef producers, rather than by general revenues. This funding mechanism, they argue, has two relevant effects: it gives control over the beef program not to politically accountable legislators, but to a narrow interest group that will pay no heed to respondents' dissenting views, and it creates the perception that the advertisements speak for beef producers such as respondents.

We reject the first point. The compelled-*subsidy* analysis is altogether unaffected by whether the funds for the promotions are raised by general taxes or through a targeted assessment. Citizens may challenge compelled support of private speech, but have no First Amendment right not to fund government speech. And that is no less true when the funding is achieved through targeted assessments devoted exclusively to the program to which the assessed citizens object. . . .

. . . The Secretary of Agriculture, a politically accountable official, oversees the program, appoints and dismisses the key personnel, and retains absolute veto power over the advertisements' content, right down to the wording. . . .

. . .

* * *

Respondents' complaint asserted a number of other grounds for declaring the Beef Act, the Beef Order, or both invalid in their entirety. The District Court, having enjoined the Act and the Order on the basis of the First Amendment, had no occasion to address these other grounds. Respondents may now proceed on these other claims. . . .

. . .

Justice Thomas, concurring.

I join the Court's opinion. I continue to believe that "[a]ny regulation that compels the funding of advertising must be subjected to the most stringent First Amendment scrutiny." . . . At the same time, I recognize that this principle must be qualified where the regulation compels the funding of speech that is the government's own. It cannot be that all taxpayers have a First Amendment objection to taxpayer-funded government speech, even if the funded speech is not "germane" to some broader regulatory program. . . .

. . .

Justice Breyer, concurring.

The beef checkoff program in these cases is virtually identical to the mushroom checkoff program in United States v. United Foods, Inc., which the Court struck down on First Amendment grounds. The "government speech" theory the Court adopts today was not before us in United Foods, and we declined to consider it when it was raised at the eleventh hour. . . .

I remain of the view that the assessments in these cases are best described as a form of economic regulation. However, I recognize that a majority of the Court does not share that view. Now that we have had an opportunity to consider the "government speech" theory, I accept it as a solution to the problem presented by these cases. With the caveat that I continue to believe that my dissent in *United Foods* offers a preferable approach, I join the Court's opinion.

Justice Ginsburg, concurring in the judgment.

I resist ranking the promotional messages ... as government speech.... I remain persuaded, however, that the assessments in these cases qualify as permissible economic regulation.... For that reason, I concur in the judgment.

Justice Kennedy, dissenting.

I join Justice Souter's dissenting opinion, which demonstrates with persuasive analysis why the speech at issue here cannot meaningfully be considered government speech at all. I would reserve for another day the difficult First Amendment questions that would arise if the government were to target a discrete group of citizens to pay even for speech that the government does "embrace as publicly as it speaks."

Justice Souter, with whom Justice Stevens and Justice Kennedy join, dissenting.

. . .

... [I]n *United Foods* ... we left open the possibility that a compelled subsidy would be justifiable not only as one element of an otherwise valid regulatory scheme, but also as speech of the Government itself, which the Government may pay for with revenue (usually from taxes) exacted from those who dissent from the message as well as from those who agree with it or do not care about it. Not surprisingly, the Government argues here that the beef advertising is its own speech, exempting it from the First Amendment bar against extracting special subsidies from those unwilling to underwrite an objectionable message.

The Court accepts the defense unwisely. The error is not that government speech can never justify compelling a subsidy, but that a compelled subsidy should not be justifiable by speech unless the government must put that speech forward as its own. Otherwise there is no check whatever on government's power to compel special speech subsidies, and the rule of *United Foods* is a dead letter. I take the view that if government relies on the government-speech doctrine to compel specific groups to fund speech with targeted taxes, it must make itself politically accountable by indicating that the content actually is a government message, not just the statement of one self-interested group the government is currently willing to invest with power. Sometimes, as in these very cases, government can make an effective disclosure only by explicitly labeling the speech as its own. Because the Beef Act fails to require the Government to show its hand, I would affirm the judgment of the Court of Appeals holding the Act unconstitutional, and I respectfully dissent from the Court's decision to condone this compelled subsidy.

. . .

The adequacy of the democratic process to render the subsidization of government speech tolerable is, naturally, tied to the character of the subsidy. For when government funds its speech with general tax revenue, as it usually does, no individual taxpayer or group of taxpayers can lay claim to a special, or even a particularly strong, connection to the money spent (and hence to the speech funded).... Outrage is likely to be rare, and disagreement tends to stay temperate. But the relative palatability of a remote subsidy shared by every taxpayer is not to be found when the speech is funded with targeted taxes. For then, as here, the particular interests of those singled out to pay the tax are closely linked with the expression, and taxpayers who disagree with it suffer a more acute limitation on their presumptive autonomy as speakers to decide what to say and what to pay for others to say....

. . .

In sum, the First Amendment cannot be implemented by sanctioning government deception by omission (or by misleading statement) of the sort the Court today condones, and expression that is not ostensibly governmental, which government is not required to embrace as publicly as it speaks, cannot constitute government speech sufficient to justify enforcement of a targeted subsidy to broadcast it. The Court of Appeals thus correctly held that *United Foods* renders the Beef Act's mandatory-assessment provisions unconstitutional.

SECTION 4. APPLICATION OF THE FIRST AMENDMENT TO GOVERNMENT REGULATION OF ELECTIONS

A. CHOOSING AND ELECTING CANDIDATES FOR PUBLIC OFFICE

Page 1616. Add at end of subsection:

Clingman v. Beaver

___ U.S. ___, 125 S.Ct. 2029, ___ L.Ed.2d ___ (2005).

Justice Thomas delivered the opinion of the Court, except as to Part II–A.

Oklahoma has a semiclosed primary system, in which a political party may invite only its own party members and voters registered as Independents to vote in the party's primary. The Court of Appeals held that this system violates the right to freedom of association of the Libertarian Party of Oklahoma (LPO) and several Oklahomans who are registered members of the Republican and Democratic parties. We hold that it does not.

I

Oklahoma's election laws provide that only registered members of a political party may vote in the party's primary ... unless the party opens its primary to registered Independents as well.... In May 2000, the LPO notified the secretary of the Oklahoma State Election Board that it wanted to open its upcoming primary to all registered Oklahoma voters, without regard to their party affiliation. . . . [T]he secretary agreed as to Independent voters, but not as to voters registered with other political parties. The LPO and several Republican and Democratic voters then sued for declaratory and injunctive relief in the United States District Court for the Western District of Oklahoma, alleging that Oklahoma's semiclosed primary law unconstitutionally burdens their First Amendment right to freedom of political association. . . .

. . . The District Court . . . upheld the semiclosed primary statute as constitutional. . . .

On appeal, the Court of Appeals for the Tenth Circuit reversed . . . . [It] concluded that the State's semiclosed primary statute imposed a severe burden on respondents' associational rights. . . . Finding none of Oklahoma's interests compelling, the Court of Appeals enjoined Oklahoma from using its semiclosed primary law. Because the Court of Appeals' decision not only prohibits Oklahoma from using its primary system but also casts doubt on the semiclosed primary laws of 23 other States, we granted certiorari. . . .

II

The Constitution grants States "broad power to prescribe the 'Time, Places and Manner of holding Elections for Senators and Representatives,' Art 1, § 4, cl. 1, which power is matched by state control over the election process for state offices." . . . We have held that the First Amendment, among other things, protects the right of citizens "to band together in promoting among the electorate candidates who espouse their political views." California Democratic Party v. Jones, 530 U.S. 567. Regulations that impose severe burdens on associational rights must be narrowly tailored to serve a compelling state interest. . . . However, when regulations impose lesser burdens, "a State's important regulatory interests will usually be enough to justify reasonable, nondiscriminatory restrictions." . . . This case presents a question . . . whether a State may prevent a political party from inviting registered voters of other parties to vote in its primary . . . We are persuaded that any burden Oklahoma's semiclosed primary imposes is minor and justified by legitimate state interests. . . .

A

At the outset, we note that Oklahoma's semiclosed primary system is unlike other laws this Court has held to infringe associational rights. Oklahoma has not sought through its electoral system to . . . compel the LPO's association with unwanted members or voters, see *Jones*, supra,. . . . The LPO is free to canvass the electorate, enroll or exclude potential members, nominate the candidate of its choice, and engage in the same electoral activities as every other political party in Oklahoma. Oklahoma merely prohibits the LPO from leaving the selection of its candidates to people who are members of another political party. . . .

In other words, the Republican and Democratic voters who have brought this action do not want to associate with the LPO, at least not in any formal sense. They wish to remain registered with the Republican, Democratic, or Reform parties, and yet to assist in selecting the Libertarian Party's candidates for the general election. Their interest is in casting a vote for a Libertarian candidate in a particular primary election, rather than in banding together with fellow citizens committed to the LPO's political goals and ideas. ... And the LPO is happy to have their votes, if not their membership on the party rolls.

However, a voter who is unwilling to disaffiliate from another party to vote in the LPO's primary forms little "association" with the LPO—nor the LPO with him....

. . .

... Oklahoma's law does not regulate the LPO's internal processes, its authority to exclude unwanted members, or its capacity to communicate with the public.... Oklahoma conditions the party's ability to welcome a voter into its primary on the voter's willingness to dissociate from his current party of choice. If anything, it is "[t]he moment of choosing the party's nominee" that matters far more, ... for that is " 'the crucial juncture at which the appeal to common principles may be translated into concerted action, and hence to political power in the community,' ".... If a party may be prevented from associating with the candidate of its choice ... because that candidate refuses to disaffiliate from another political party, a party may also be prevented from associating with a voter who refuses to do the same....

. . .

B

. . .

... To deem ordinary and widespread burdens like these severe would subject virtually every electoral regulation to strict scrutiny, hamper the ability of States to run efficient and equitable elections, and compel federal courts to rewrite state electoral codes. The Constitution does not require that result, for it is beyond question "that States may, and inevitably must, enact reasonable regulations of parties, elections, and ballots to reduce election-and campaign-related disorder." ...

C

When a state electoral provision places no heavy burden on associational rights, "a State's important regulatory interests will usually be enough to justify reasonable, nondiscriminatory restrictions." ... Here, Oklahoma's semiclosed primary advances a number of regulatory interests that this Court recognizes as important: It "preserv[es] [political] parties as viable and identifiable interest groups," ... enhances parties' electioneering and party-building efforts, ... and guards against party raiding and "sore loser" candidacies by spurned primary contenders.... It does not matter that the LPO is willing to risk the surrender of its identity in exchange for electoral success. Oklahoma's interest is independent and concerns the integrity of its primary system. The State wants to "avoid primary election outcomes which would tend to confuse or mislead the general voting population to the extent [it] relies on party labels as representative of certain ideologies." ... Oklahoma reasonably has concluded that opening the LPO's primary to all voters regardless of party affiliation would undermine the crucial role of political parties in the primary process. Cf. *Jones*, 530 U.S., at 574.

. . .

* * *

Oklahoma remains free to allow the LPO to invite registered voters of other parties to vote in its primary. But the Constitution leaves that choice to the democratic process, not to the courts. . . .

Justice O'Connor, with whom Justice Breyer joins except as to Part III, concurring in part and concurring in the judgment.

I join the Court's opinion except for Part II–A. Although I agree with most of the Court's reasoning, I write separately to emphasize two points. First, I think respondents' claim implicates important associational interests, and I see no reason to minimize those interests to dispose of this case. Second, I agree with the Court that only Oklahoma's semiclosed primary law is properly before us, that standing alone it imposes only a modest, nondiscriminatory burden on respondents' associational rights, and that this burden is justified by the State's legitimate regulatory interests. I note, however, that there are some grounds for concern that other state laws may unreasonably restrict voters' ability to change party registration so as to participate in the Libertarian Party of Oklahoma's (LPO) primary. A realistic assessment of regulatory burdens on associational rights would, in an appropriate case, require examination of the cumulative effects of the State's overall scheme governing primary elections; and any finding of a more severe burden would trigger more probing review of the justifications offered by the State.

. . .

. . . [W]here a party invites a voter to participate in its primary and the voter seeks to do so, we should begin with the premise that there are significant associational interests at stake. From this starting point, we can then ask to what extent and in what manner the State may justifiably restrict those interests.

. . .

Justice Stevens, with whom Justice Ginsburg joins, and with whom Justice Souter joins as to Parts I, II, and III, dissenting.

The Court's decision today diminishes the value of two important rights protected by the First Amendment: the individual citizen's right to vote for the candidate of her choice and a political party's right to define its own mission. No one would contend that a citizen's membership in either the Republican or the Democratic Party could disqualify her from attending political functions sponsored by another party, or from voting for a third party's candidate in a general election. If a third party invites her to participate in its primary election, her right to support the candidate of her choice merits constitutional protection, whether she elects to make a speech, to donate funds, or to cast a ballot. The importance of vindicating that individual right far outweighs any public interest in punishing registered Republicans or Democrats for acts of disloyalty. The balance becomes even more lopsided when the individual right is reinforced by the right of the Libertarian Party of Oklahoma (LPO) to associate with willing voters.

In concluding that the State's interests override those important values, the Court focuses on interests that are not legitimate. States do not have a valid interest in manipulating the outcome of elections, in protecting the major parties from competition, or in stunting the growth of new parties. While States do have a valid interest in conducting orderly elections and in encouraging the maximum participation of voters, neither of these interests overrides (or, indeed, even conflicts with) the valid interests of both the LPO and the voters who wish to participate in its primary.

In the final analysis, this case is simple.... Oklahoma ... denies a party the right to invite willing voters to participate in its primary elections. I would therefore affirm the Court of Appeals' judgment.

CHAPTER 17

RELIGION AND THE CONSTITUTION

SECTION 1. THE ESTABLISHMENT CLAUSE

B. GOVERNMENT RELIGIOUS EXERCISES, CEREMONIES, DISPLAYS, AND PRACTICES

2. RELIGIOUS SPEECH AND DISPLAYS ON PUBLIC PROPERTY

Page 1748. Replace County of Allegheny v. American Civil Liberties Union:

McCreary County, Kentucky v. American Civil Liberties Union of Kentucky

___ U.S. ___, 125 S.Ct. 2722, ___ L.Ed.2d ___ (2005).

Justice Souter delivered the opinion of the Court.

Executives of two counties posted a version of the Ten Commandments on the walls of their courthouses. After suits were filed charging violations of the Establishment Clause, the legislative body of each county adopted a resolution calling for a more extensive exhibit meant to show that the Commandments are Kentucky's "precedent legal code." The result in each instance was a modified display of the Commandments surrounded by texts containing religious references as their sole common element. After changing counsel, the counties revised the exhibits again by eliminating some documents, expanding the text set out in another, and adding some new ones.

The issues are whether a determination of the counties' purpose is a sound basis for ruling on the Establishment Clause complaints, and whether evaluation of the counties' claim of secular purpose for the ultimate displays may take their evolution into account. We hold that the counties' manifest objective may be dispositive of the constitutional enquiry, and that the development of the presentation should be considered when determining its purpose.

I

. . .

In November 1999, respondents ... sued the Counties in Federal District Court ... and sought a preliminary injunction against maintaining the displays, which the ACLU charged were violations of the prohibition of religious establishment included in the First Amendment of the Constitution. Within a month, and before the District Court had responded to the request for injunction, the legislative body of each County authorized a second, expanded display, by nearly identical resolutions reciting that the Ten Commandments are "the precedent legal code upon which the civil and criminal codes of ... Kentucky are founded," and stating several grounds for taking that position: that "the Ten Commandments are codified in Kentucky's civil and criminal laws"; that the Kentucky House of Representatives had in 1993 "voted unanimously ... to adjourn ... 'in remembrance and honor of Jesus Christ, the Prince of Ethics' "; that the "County Judge and ... magistrates agree with the arguments set out by Judge [Roy] Moore" in defense of his "display [of] the Ten Commandments in his courtroom"; and that the "Founding Father[s] [had an] explicit understanding of the duty of elected officials to publicly acknowledge God as the source of America's strength and direction."

As directed by the resolutions, the Counties expanded the displays of the Ten Commandments in their locations, presumably along with copies of the resolution, which instructed that it, too, be posted. In addition to the first display's large framed copy of the edited King James version of the Commandments, the second included eight other documents in smaller frames, each either having a religious theme or excerpted to highlight a religious element. The documents were the "endowed by their Creator" passage from the Declaration of Independence; the Preamble to the Constitution of Kentucky; the national motto, "In God We Trust"; a page from the Congressional Record of February 2, 1983, proclaiming the Year of the Bible and including a statement of the Ten Commandments; a proclamation by President Abraham Lincoln designating April 30, 1863, a National Day of Prayer and Humiliation; an excerpt from President Lincoln's "Reply to Loyal Colored People of Baltimore upon Presentation of a Bible," reading that "[t]he Bible is the best gift God has ever given to man"; a proclamation by President Reagan marking 1983 the Year of the Bible; and the Mayflower Compact.

After argument, the District Court entered a preliminary injunction on May 5, 2000, ordering that the "display ... be removed from [each] County Courthouse IMMEDIATELY" and that no county official "erect or cause to be erected similar displays." ... As to governmental purpose, it concluded that the original display "lack[ed] any secular purpose" because the Commandments "are a distinctly religious document...." The court found that the second version also "clearly lack[ed] a secular purpose" because the "Count[ies] narrowly tailored [their] selection of foundational documents to incorporate only those with specific references to Christianity."

The Counties ... voluntarily dismissed [their appeal] after hiring new lawyers. They then installed another display in each courthouse, the third within a year. No new resolution authorized this one, nor did the Counties repeal the resolutions that preceded the second. The posting consists of nine framed documents of equal size, one of them setting out the Ten Commandments explicitly identified as the "King James Version" at Exodus 20:3–17 and quoted at greater length than before.... Assembled with the Commandments are framed copies of the Magna Carta, the Declaration of Independence, the Bill of Rights, the lyrics of the Star Spangled Banner, the Mayflower Compact, the National Motto, the Preamble to the Kentucky Constitution, and a picture of Lady Justice. The collection is entitled "The Foundations of American Law and Government Display" and each document comes with a statement about its historical and legal significance. The comment on the Ten Commandments reads:

> "The Ten Commandments have profoundly influenced the formation of Western legal thought and the formation of our country. That influence is clearly seen in the Declaration of Independence, which declared that 'We hold these truths to be self-evident, that all men are created equal, that they are endowed by their Creator with certain unalienable Rights, that among these are Life, Liberty, and the pursuit of Happiness.' The Ten Commandments provide the moral background of the Declaration of Independence and the foundation of our legal tradition."

The ACLU moved to supplement the preliminary injunction to enjoin the Counties' third display, and the Counties responded with several explanations for the new version, including desires "to demonstrate that the Ten Commandments were part of the foundation of American Law and Government" and "to educate the citizens of the county regarding some of the documents that played a significant role in the foundation of our system of law and government." ... The court, however, took the objective of proclaiming the Commandments' foundational value as "a religious, rather than secular, purpose" ... and found that the assertion that the Counties' broader educational goals are secular "crumble[s] ... upon an examination of the history of this litigation,"

... As requested, the trial court supplemented the injunction, and a divided panel of the Court of Appeals for the Sixth Circuit affirmed....

We ... now affirm.

II

Twenty-five years ago in a case prompted by posting the Ten Commandments in Kentucky's public schools, this Court recognized that the Commandments "are undeniably a sacred text in the Jewish and Christian faiths" and held that their display in public classrooms violated the First Amendment's bar against establishment of religion. Stone [v. Graham] 449 U.S., at 41. *Stone* found a predominantly religious purpose in the government's posting of the Commandments, given their prominence as " 'an instrument of religion,' " .... The Counties ask for a different approach here by arguing that official purpose is unknowable and the search for it inherently vain. In the alternative, the Counties would avoid the District Court's conclusion by having us limit the scope of the purpose enquiry so severely that any trivial rationalization would suffice, under a standard oblivious to the history of religious government action like the progression of exhibits in this case.

A

Ever since Lemon v. Kurtzman summarized the three familiar considerations for evaluating Establishment Clause claims, looking to whether government action has "a secular legislative purpose" has been a common, albeit seldom dispositive, element of our cases.... Though we have found government action motivated by an illegitimate purpose only four times since *Lemon*, and "the secular purpose requirement alone may rarely be determinative ... , it nevertheless serves an important function." ...

The touchstone for our analysis is the principle that the "First Amendment mandates governmental neutrality between religion and religion, and between religion and nonreligion." ... When the government acts with the ostensible and predominant purpose of advancing religion, it violates that central Establishment Clause value of official religious neutrality, there being no neutrality when the government's ostensible object is to take sides.... By showing a purpose to favor religion, the government "sends the ... message to ... nonadherents 'that they are outsiders, not full members of the political community, and an accompanying message to adherents that they are insiders, favored members' "....

. . .

B

Despite the intuitive importance of official purpose to the realization of Establishment Clause values, the Counties ask us to abandon *Lemon* 's purpose test, or at least to truncate any enquiry into purpose here. Their first argument is that the very consideration of purpose is deceptive: according to them, true "purpose" is unknowable, and its search merely an excuse for courts to act selectively and unpredictably in picking out evidence of subjective intent. The assertions are as seismic as they are unconvincing.

Examination of purpose is a staple of statutory interpretation that makes up the daily fare of every appellate court in the country, ... and governmental purpose is a key element of a good deal of constitutional doctrine, e.g., Washington v. Davis, 426 U.S. 229.... With enquiries into purpose this common, if they were nothing but hunts for mares' nests deflecting attention from bare judicial will, the whole notion of purpose in law would have dropped into disrepute long ago.

But scrutinizing purpose does make practical sense, as in Establishment Clause analysis, where an understanding of official objective emerges from readily discoverable fact, without any judicial psychoanalysis of a drafter's heart of hearts.... There is, then, nothing hinting at an unpredictable or disingenuous exercise when a court enquires into purpose after a claim is raised under the Establishment Clause.

The cases with findings of a predominantly religious purpose point to the straightforward nature of the test.... [I]n *Stone*, the Court held that the "[p]osting of religious texts on the wall serve[d] no ... educational function," and found that if "the posted copies of the Ten Commandments [were] to have any effect at all, it [would] be to induce the schoolchildren to read, meditate upon, perhaps to venerate and obey, the Commandments." ...

Nor is there any indication that the enquiry is rigged in practice to finding a religious purpose dominant every time a case is filed. In the past, the test has not been fatal very often, presumably because government does not generally act unconstitutionally, with the predominant purpose of advancing religion. That said, one consequence of the corollary that Establishment Clause analysis does not look to the veiled psyche of government officers could be that in some of the cases in which establishment complaints failed, savvy officials had disguised their religious intent so cleverly that the objective observer just missed it. But that is no reason for great constitutional concern. If someone in the government hides religious motive so well that the " 'objective observer, acquainted with the text, legislative history, and implementation of the statute,' " ... cannot see it, then without something more the government does not make a divisive announcement that in itself amounts to taking religious sides. A secret motive stirs up no strife and does nothing to make outsiders of nonadherents, and it suffices to wait and see whether such government action turns out to have (as it may even be likely to have) the illegitimate effect of advancing religion.

C

After declining the invitation to abandon concern with purpose wholesale, we also have to avoid the Counties' alternative tack of trivializing the enquiry into it. The Counties would read the cases as if the purpose enquiry were so naive that any transparent claim to secularity would satisfy it, and they would cut context out of the enquiry, to the point of ignoring history, no matter what bearing it actually had on the significance of current circumstances. There is no precedent for the Counties' arguments, or reason supporting them.

1

. . .

... [W]e have not made the purpose test a pushover for any secular claim.... [I]n those unusual cases where the claim was an apparent sham, or the secular purpose secondary, the unsurprising results have been findings of no adequate secular object, as against a predominantly religious one.

2

The Counties' second proffered limitation can be dispatched quickly. They argue that purpose in a case like this one should be inferred, if at all, only from the latest news about the last in a series of governmental actions, however close they may all be in time and subject. But the world is not made brand new every morning, and the Counties are simply asking us to ignore perfectly probative evidence; they want an absentminded objective observer, not one presumed to be familiar with the history of the government's actions and competent to learn what history has to show....

III

. . .

We take *Stone* as the initial legal benchmark, our only case dealing with the constitutionality of displaying the Commandments. *Stone* recognized that the Commandments are an "instrument of religion" and that, at least on the facts before it, the display of their text could presumptively be understood as meant to advance religion: although state law specifically required their posting in public school classrooms, their isolated exhibition did not leave room even for an argument that secular education explained their being there.... But *Stone* did not purport to decide the constitutionality of every possible way the Commandments might be set out by the government, and under the Establishment Clause detail is key....

A

The display rejected in *Stone* had two obvious similarities to the first one in the sequence here: both set out a text of the Commandments as distinct from any traditionally symbolic representation, and each stood alone, not part of an arguably secular display. *Stone* stressed the significance of integrating the Commandments into a secular scheme to forestall the broadcast of an otherwise clearly religious message, ... and for good reason, the Commandments being a central point of reference in the religious and moral history of Jews and Christians. They proclaim the existence of a monotheistic god (no other gods). They regulate details of religious obligation (no graven images, no sabbath breaking, no vain oath swearing). And they unmistakably rest even the universally accepted prohibitions (as against murder, theft, and the like) on the sanction of the divinity proclaimed at the beginning of the text. Displaying that text is thus different from a symbolic depiction, like tablets with 10 roman numerals, which could be seen as alluding to a general notion of law, not a sectarian conception of faith.... Actually, the posting by the Counties lacked even the *Stone* display's implausible disclaimer that the Commandments were set out to show their effect on the civil law. What is more, at the ceremony for posting the framed Commandments in Pulaski County, the county executive was accompanied by his pastor, who testified to the certainty of the existence of God. The reasonable observer could only think that the Counties meant to emphasize and celebrate the Commandments' religious message.

This is not to deny that the Commandments have had influence on civil or secular law; a major text of a majority religion is bound to be felt. The point is simply that the original text viewed in its entirety is an unmistakably religious statement dealing with religious obligations and with morality subject to religious sanction. When the government initiates an effort to place this statement alone in public view, a religious object is unmistakable.

B

Once the Counties were sued, they modified the exhibits and invited additional insight into their purpose in a display that hung for about six months. This new one was the product of forthright and nearly identical Pulaski and McCreary County resolutions listing a series of American historical documents with theistic and Christian references, which were to be posted in order to furnish a setting for displaying the Ten Commandments and any "other Kentucky and American historical documen[t]" without raising concern about "any Christian or religious references" in them.... [T]he resolutions expressed support for an Alabama judge who posted the Commandments in his courtroom, and cited the fact the Kentucky Legislature once adjourned a session in honor of "Jesus Christ, Prince of Ethics." ...

In this second display, unlike the first, the Commandments were not hung in isolation, merely leaving the Counties' purpose to emerge from the pervasively religious text of the Commandments themselves. Instead, the second version was required to include the statement of the government's purpose expressly set out in the county resolutions, and underscored it by juxtaposing the Commandments to other documents with highlighted references to God as their sole common element. The display's unstinting focus was on religious passages, showing that the Counties were posting the Commandments precisely because of their sectarian content. That demonstration of the government's objective was enhanced by serial religious references and the accompanying resolution's claim about the embodiment of ethics in Christ. Together, the display and resolution presented an indisputable, and undisputed, showing of an impermissible purpose.

. . .

C

1

After the Counties changed lawyers, they mounted a third display, without a new resolution or repeal of the old one. The result was the "Foundations of American Law and Government" exhibit, which placed the Commandments in the company of other documents the Counties thought especially significant in the historical foundation of American government. In trying to persuade the District Court to lift the preliminary injunction, the Counties cited several new purposes for the third version, including a desire "to educate the citizens of the county regarding some of the documents that played a significant role in the foundation of our system of law and government." The Counties' claims did not, however, persuade the court, intimately familiar with the details of this litigation, or the Court of Appeals, neither of which found a legitimizing secular purpose in this third version of the display. " 'When both courts [that have already passed on the case] are unable to discern an arguably valid secular purpose, this Court normally should hesitate to find one.' "

[N]ew statements of purpose were presented only as a litigating position, there being no further authorizing action by the Counties' governing boards. And although repeal of the earlier county authorizations would not have erased them from the record of evidence bearing on current purpose, the extraordinary resolutions for the second display passed just months earlier were not repealed or otherwise repudiated. Indeed, the sectarian spirit of the common resolution found enhanced expression in the third display, which quoted more of the purely religious language of the Commandments than the first two displays had done. . . .

. . .

2

In holding the preliminary injunction adequately supported by evidence that the Counties' purpose had not changed at the third stage, we do not decide that the Counties' past actions forever taint any effort on their part to deal with the subject matter. We hold only that purpose needs to be taken seriously under the Establishment Clause and needs to be understood in light of context; an implausible claim that governmental purpose has changed should not carry the day in a court of law any more than in a head with common sense. It is enough to say here that district courts are fully capable of adjusting preliminary relief to take account of genuine changes in constitutionally significant conditions. . . .

Nor do we have occasion here to hold that a sacred text can never be integrated constitutionally into a governmental display on the subject of law, or American history. We do not forget, and in this litigation have frequently been reminded, that our own courtroom frieze was deliberately designed in the exercise of governmental authority so as to include the figure of Moses holding tablets exhibiting a portion of the Hebrew text of the later, secularly phrased Commandments; in the company of 17 other lawgivers, most of them secular figures, there is no risk that Moses would strike an observer as evidence that the National Government was violating neutrality in religion.

IV

The importance of neutrality as an interpretive guide is no less true now than it was when the Court broached the principle in *Everson* . . . and a word needs to be said about the different view taken in today's dissent. We all agree, of course, on the need for some interpretative help. The First Amendment contains no textual definition of "establishment," and the term is certainly not self-defining. No one contends that the prohibition of establishment stops at a designation of a national (or with Fourteenth Amendment incorporation, . . . a state) church, but nothing in the text says just how much more it covers. There is no simple answer, for more than one reason.

The prohibition on establishment covers a variety of issues from prayer in widely varying government settings, to financial aid for religious individuals and institutions, to comment on religious questions. In these varied settings, issues about interpreting inexact Establishment Clause language, like difficult interpretative issues generally, arise from the tension of competing values, each constitutionally respectable, but none open to realization to the logical limit.

The First Amendment has not one but two clauses tied to "religion," the second forbidding any prohibition on the "the free exercise thereof," and sometimes, the two clauses compete: spending government money on the clergy looks like establishing religion, but if the government cannot pay for military chaplains a good many soldiers and sailors would be kept from the opportunity to exercise their chosen religions. . . . At other times, limits on governmental action that might make sense as a way to avoid establishment could arguably limit freedom of speech when the speaking is done under government auspices. . . . The dissent, then, is wrong to read cases like Walz v. Tax Comm'n of City of New York, 397 U.S. 664 (1970), as a rejection of neutrality on its own terms, for trade-offs are inevitable, and an elegant interpretative rule to draw the line in all the multifarious situations is not be had.

Given the variety of interpretative problems, the principle of neutrality has provided a good sense of direction: the government may not favor one religion over another, or religion over irreligion, religious choice being the prerogative of individuals under the Free Exercise Clause. . . . A sense of the past thus points to governmental neutrality as an objective of the Establishment Clause, and a sensible standard for applying it. To be sure, given its generality as a principle, an appeal to neutrality alone cannot possibly lay every issue to rest, or tell us what issues on the margins are substantial enough for constitutional significance, a point that has been clear from the Founding era to modern times. . . .

The dissent, however, puts forward a limitation on the application of the neutrality principle, with citations to historical evidence said to show that the Framers understood the ban on establishment of religion as sufficiently narrow to allow the government to espouse submission to the divine will. The dissent identifies God as the God of monotheism, all of whose three principal strains (Jewish, Christian, and Muslim) acknowledge the religious importance of the Ten Commandments. On the dissent's view, it apparently follows that even rigorous espousal of a common element of this common monotheism, is consistent with the establishment ban.

But the dissent's argument for the original understanding is flawed from the outset by its failure to consider the full range of evidence showing what the Framers believed. The dissent is certainly correct in putting forward evidence that some of the Framers thought some endorsement of religion was compatible with the establishment ban; the dissent quotes the first President as stating that "national morality [cannot] prevail in exclusion of religious principle," for example, and it cites his first Thanksgiving proclamation giving thanks to God.... Surely if expressions like these from Washington and his contemporaries were all we had to go on, there would be a good case that the neutrality principle has the effect of broadening the ban on establishment beyond the Framers' understanding of it (although there would, of course, still be the question of whether the historical case could overcome some 60 years of precedent taking neutrality as its guiding principle).

But the fact is that we do have more to go on, for there is also evidence supporting the proposition that the Framers intended the Establishment Clause to require governmental neutrality in matters of religion, including neutrality in statements acknowledging religion. The very language of the Establishment Clause represented a significant departure from early drafts that merely prohibited a single national religion, and, the final language instead "extended [the] prohibition to state support for 'religion' in general." ...

The historical record, moreover, is complicated beyond the dissent's account by the writings and practices of figures no less influential than Thomas Jefferson and James Madison. Jefferson, for example, refused to issue Thanksgiving Proclamations because he believed that they violated the Constitution....

The fair inference is that there was no common understanding about the limits of the establishment prohibition, and the dissent's conclusion that its narrower view was the original understanding, stretches the evidence beyond tensile capacity. What the evidence does show is a group of statesmen, like others before and after them, who proposed a guarantee with contours not wholly worked out, leaving the Establishment Clause with edges still to be determined. And none the worse for that. Indeterminate edges are the kind to have in a constitution meant to endure, and to meet "exigencies which, if foreseen at all, must have been seen dimly, and which can be best provided for as they occur." ...

While the dissent fails to show a consistent original understanding from which to argue that the neutrality principle should be rejected, it does manage to deliver a surprise. As mentioned, the dissent says that the deity the Framers had in mind was the God of monotheism, with the consequence that government may espouse a tenet of traditional monotheism. This is truly a remarkable view. Other members of the Court have dissented on the ground that the Establishment Clause bars nothing more than governmental preference for one religion over another ... , but at least religion has previously been treated inclusively. Today's dissent, however, apparently means that government should be free to approve the core beliefs of a favored religion over the tenets of others, a view that should trouble anyone who prizes religious liberty. Certainly history cannot justify it; on the contrary, history shows that the religion of concern to the Framers was not that of the monotheistic faiths generally, but Christianity in particular, a fact that no member of this Court takes as a premise for construing the Religion Clauses.... [T]here is, it seems, no escape from interpretative consequences that would surprise the Framers. Thus, it appears to be common ground in the interpretation of a Constitution "intended to endure for ages to come," ... that applications unanticipated by the Framers are inevitable.

Historical evidence thus supports no solid argument for changing course ... [T]he divisiveness of religion in current public life is inescapable. This is no time to deny the prudence of understanding the Establishment Clause to require the Government to stay neutral on religious belief, which is reserved for the conscience of the individual.

V

Given the ample support for the District Court's finding of a predominantly religious purpose behind the Counties' third display, we affirm the Sixth Circuit in upholding the preliminary injunction.

. . .

Justice O'Connor, concurring.

I join in the Court's opinion....

Reasonable minds can disagree about how to apply the Religion Clauses in a given case. But the goal of the Clauses is clear: to carry out the Founders' plan of preserving religious liberty to the fullest extent possible in a pluralistic society. By enforcing the Clauses, we have kept religion a matter for the individual conscience, not for the prosecutor or bureaucrat. At a time when we see around the world the violent consequences of the assumption of religious authority by government, Americans may count themselves fortunate: Our regard for constitutional boundaries has protected us from similar travails, while allowing private religious exercise to flourish....

. . .

Given the history of this particular display of the Ten Commandments, the Court correctly finds an Establishment Clause violation. The purpose behind the counties' display is relevant because it conveys an unmistakable message of endorsement to the reasonable observer....

. . .

Justice Scalia, with whom the Chief Justice and Justice Thomas join, and with whom Justice Kennedy joins as to Parts II and III, dissenting.

I would uphold McCreary County and Pulaski County, Kentucky's (hereinafter Counties) displays of the Ten Commandments. I shall discuss first, why the Court's oft repeated assertion that the government cannot favor religious practice is false; second, why today's opinion extends the scope of that falsehood even beyond prior cases; and third, why even on the basis of the Court's false assumptions the judgment here is wrong.

I

. . .

. . . [Absolutely forbidding a Head of State to invoke God's blessing] is one model of the relationship between church and state—a model spread across Europe by the armies of Napoleon, and reflected in the Constitution of France, which begins "France is [a] . . . secular Republic." . . . This is not, and never was, the model adopted by America. . . .

. . .

Nor have the views of our people on this matter significantly changed. Presidents continue to conclude the Presidential oath with the words "so help me God." Our legislatures, state and national, continue to open their sessions with prayer led by official chaplains. The sessions of this Court continue to open with the prayer "God save the United States and this Honorable Court." Invocation of the Almighty by our public figures, at all levels of government, remains commonplace. Our coinage bears the motto "IN GOD WE TRUST." And our Pledge of Allegiance contains the acknowledgment that we are a Nation "under God." . . .

With all of this reality (and much more) staring it in the face, how can the Court *possibly* assert that " 'the First Amendment mandates governmental neutrality between . . . religion and nonreligion,' " and that "[m]anifesting a purpose to favor . . . adherence to religion generally," is unconstitutional? Who says so? Surely not the words of the Constitution. Surely not the history and traditions that reflect our society's constant understanding of those words. Surely not even the current sense of our society, recently reflected in an Act of Congress adopted *unanimously* by the Senate and with only 5 nays in the House of Representatives, . . . criticizing a Court of Appeals opinion that had held "under God" in the Pledge of Allegiance unconstitutional. . . . And it is, moreover, a thoroughly discredited say-so. It is discredited, to begin with, because a majority of the Justices on the current Court (including at least one Member of today's majority) have, in separate opinions, repudiated the brain-spun "*Lemon* test" that embodies the supposed principle of neutrality between religion and irreligion. . . . And it is discredited because the Court has not had the courage (or the foolhardiness) to apply the neutrality principle consistently.

What distinguishes the rule of law from the dictatorship of a shifting Supreme Court majority is the absolutely indispensable requirement that judicial opinions be grounded in consistently applied principle. That is what prevents judges from ruling now this way, now that—thumbs up or thumbs down—as their personal preferences dictate. Today's opinion forthrightly (or actually, somewhat less than forthrightly) admits that it does not rest upon consistently applied principle. . . . [T]he Court acknowledges that the "Establishment Clause doctrine" it purports to be applying "lacks the comfort of categorical absolutes." What the Court means by this lovely euphemism is that sometimes the Court chooses to decide cases on the principle that government cannot favor religion, and sometimes it does not. The footnote goes on to say that "[i]n special instances we have found good reason" to dispense with the principle, but "[n]o such reasons present themselves here." ... It does not identify all of those "special instances," much less identify the "good reason" for their existence.

. . .

Besides appealing to the demonstrably false principle that the government cannot favor religion over irreligion, today's opinion suggests that the posting of the Ten Commandments violates the principle that the government cannot favor one religion over another.... That is indeed a valid principle where public aid or assistance to religion is concerned, ... or where the free exercise of religion is at issue, but it necessarily applies in a more limited sense to public acknowledgment of the Creator. If religion in the public forum had to be entirely nondenominational, there could be no religion in the public forum at all. One cannot say the word "God," or "the Almighty," one cannot offer public supplication or thanksgiving, without contradicting the beliefs of some people that there are many gods, or that God or the gods pay no attention to human affairs. With respect to public acknowledgment of religious belief, it is entirely clear from our Nation's historical practices that the Establishment Clause permits this disregard of polytheists and believers in unconcerned deities, just as it permits the disregard of devout atheists....

Historical practices thus demonstrate that there is a distance between the acknowledgment of a single Creator and the establishment of a religion....

B

. . .

II

As bad as the *Lemon* test is, it is worse for the fact that, since its inception, its seemingly simple mandates have been manipulated to fit whatever result the Court aimed to achieve. Today's opinion is no different. In two respects it modifies *Lemon* to ratchet up the Court's hostility to religion. First, the Court justifies inquiry into legislative purpose, not as an end itself, but as a means to ascertain the appearance of the government action to an " 'objective observer.' " Because in the Court's view the true danger to be guarded against is that the objective observer would feel like an "outside[r]" or "not [a] full membe[r] of the political community," its inquiry focuses not on the *actual purpose* of government action, but the "purpose apparent from government action." Under this approach, even if a government could show that its actual purpose was not to advance religion, it would presumably violate the Constitution as long as the Court's objective observer would think otherwise....

I have remarked before that it is an odd jurisprudence that bases the unconstitutionality of a government practice that does not *actually* advance religion on the hopes of the government that it *would* do so.... But that oddity pales in comparison to the one invited by today's analysis: the legitimacy of a government action with a wholly secular effect would turn on the *misperception* of an imaginary observer that the government officials behind the action had the intent to advance religion.

... *Lemon*'s more limited requirement ... finds no support in our cases. In all but one of the five cases in which this Court has invalidated a government practice on the basis of its purpose to benefit religion, it has first declared that the statute was motivated entirely by the desire to advance religion. . . . In Edwards [v. Aguillard, 482 U.S. 578 (1987)], the Court did say that the state action was invalid because its "primary" or "preeminent" purpose was to advance a particular religious belief, . . . but that statement was unnecessary to the result, since the Court rejected the State's only proffered secular purpose as a sham. . . .

. . .

III

Even accepting the Court's *Lemon*-based premises, the displays at issue here were constitutional.

A

To any person who happened to walk down the hallway of the McCreary or Pulaski County Courthouse during the roughly nine months when the Foundations Displays were exhibited, the displays must have seemed unremarkable—if indeed they were noticed at all. The walls of both courthouses were already lined with historical documents and other assorted portraits; each Foundations Display was exhibited in the same format as these other displays and nothing in the record suggests that either County took steps to give it greater prominence.

Entitled "The Foundations of American Law and Government Display," each display consisted of nine equally sized documents: the original version of the Magna Carta, the Declaration of Independence, the Bill of Rights, the Star Spangled Banner, the Mayflower Compact of 1620, a picture of Lady Justice, the National Motto of the United States ("In God We Trust"), the Preamble to the Kentucky Constitution, and the Ten Commandments. The displays did not emphasize any of the nine documents in any way: The frame holding the Ten Commandments was of the same size and had the same appearance as that which held each of the other documents. . . .

Posted with the documents was a plaque, identifying the display, and explaining that it "contains documents that played a significant role in the foundation of our system of law and government." . . . The explanation related to the Ten Commandments was third in the list of nine and did not serve to distinguish it from the other documents. . . .

B

On its face, the Foundations Displays manifested the purely secular purpose that the Counties asserted before the District Court: "to display documents that played a significant role in the foundation of our system of law and government." . . .

. . .

C

In any event, the Court's conclusion that the Counties exhibited the Foundations Displays with the purpose of promoting religion is doubtful. In the Court's view, the impermissible motive was apparent from the initial displays of the Ten Commandments all by themselves: When that occurs, the Court says, "a religious object is unmistakable." Surely that cannot be. If, as discussed above, the Commandments have a proper place in our civic history, even placing them by themselves can be civically motivated—especially when they are placed, not in a school (as they were in the *Stone* case upon which the Court places such reliance), but in a courthouse....

... What Justice Kennedy said of the creche in *Allegheny County* is equally true of the Counties' original Ten Commandments displays:

"No one was compelled to observe or participate in any religious ceremony or activity. [T]he count[ies] [did not] contribut[e] significant amounts of tax money to serve the cause of one religious faith. [The Ten Commandments] are purely passive symbols of [the religious foundation for many of our laws and governmental institutions]. Passersby who disagree with the message conveyed by th[e] displays are free to ignore them, or even to turn their backs, just as they are free to do when they disagree with any other form of government speech." 492 U.S., at 664....

Nor is it the case that a solo display of the Ten Commandments advances any one faith. They are assuredly a religious symbol, but they are not so closely associated with a single religious belief that their display can reasonably be understood as preferring one religious sect over another. The Ten Commandments are recognized by Judaism, Christianity, and Islam alike as divinely given....

. . .

Turning at last to the displays actually at issue in this case, the Court faults the Counties for not *repealing* the resolution expressing what the Court believes to be an impermissible intent. Under these circumstances, the Court says, "no reasonable observer could swallow the claim that the Counties had cast off the objective so unmistakable in the earlier displays." Even were I to accept all that the Court has said before, I would not agree with that assessment. To begin with, of course, it is unlikely that a reasonable observer *would even have been aware* of the resolutions, so there would be nothing to "cast off." The Court implies that the Counties may have been able to remedy the "taint" from the old resolutions by enacting a new one. But that action would have been wholly unnecessary in light of the explanation that the Counties included *with the displays themselves:* A plaque next to the documents informed all who passed by that each display "contains documents that played a significant role in the foundation of our system of law and government." Additionally, there was no reason for the Counties to repeal or repudiate the resolutions adopted with the hanging of the second displays, since they related *only to the second displays.* After complying with the District Court's order to remove the second displays "immediately," and erecting new displays that in content and by express assertion reflected a different purpose from that identified in the resolutions, the Counties had no reason to believe that their previous resolutions would be deemed to be the basis for their actions. After the Counties discovered that the sentiments expressed in the resolutions could be attributed to their most recent displays (in oral argument before this Court), they repudiated them immediately.

In sum: The first displays did not necessarily evidence an intent to further religious practice; nor did the second displays, or the resolutions authorizing them; and there is in any event no basis for attributing whatever intent motivated the first and second displays to the third. Given the presumption of regularity that always accompanies our review of official action, the Court has identified no evidence of a purpose to advance religion in a way that is inconsistent with our cases. The Court may well be correct in identifying the third displays as the fruit of a desire to display the Ten Commandments but neither our cases nor our history support its assertion that such a desire renders the fruit poisonous.

* * *

For the foregoing reasons, I would reverse the judgment of the Court of Appeals.

Van Orden v. Perry

___ U.S. ___, 125 S.Ct. 2584. ___ L.Ed.2d ___ (2005).

Chief Justice Rehnquist announced the judgment of the Court and delivered an opinion, in which Justice Scalia, Justice Kennedy, and Justice Thomas join.

The question here is whether the Establishment Clause of the First Amendment allows the display of a monument inscribed with the Ten Commandments on the Texas State Capitol grounds. We hold that it does.

The 22 acres surrounding the Texas State Capitol contain 17 monuments and 21 historical markers commemorating the "people, ideals, and events that compose Texan identity."... The monolith challenged here stands 6-feet high and 3 1/2-feet wide. It is located to the north of the Capitol building, between the Capitol and the Supreme Court building. Its primary content is the text of the Ten Commandments. An eagle grasping the American flag, an eye inside of a pyramid, and two small tablets with what appears to be an ancient script are carved above the text of the Ten Commandments. Below the text are two Stars of David and the superimposed Greek letters Chi and Rho, which represent Christ. The bottom of the monument bears the inscription "PRESENTED TO THE PEOPLE AND YOUTH OF TEXAS BY THE FRATERNAL ORDER OF EAGLES OF TEXAS 1961." ...

The legislative record surrounding the State's acceptance of the monument from the Eagles—a national social, civic, and patriotic organization—is limited to legislative journal entries. After the monument was accepted, the State selected a site for the monument based on the recommendation of the state organization responsible for maintaining the Capitol grounds. The Eagles paid the cost of erecting the monument, the dedication of which was presided over by two state legislators.

Petitioner Thomas Van Orden is a native Texan and a resident of Austin. At one time he was a licensed lawyer, having graduated from Southern Methodist Law School....

Forty years after the monument's erection and six years after Van Orden began to encounter the monument frequently, he sued numerous state officials . . . seeking both a declaration that the monument's placement violates the Establishment Clause and an injunction requiring its removal. After a bench trial, the District Court held that the monument did not contravene the Establishment Clause. It found that the State had a valid secular purpose in recognizing and commending the Eagles for their efforts to reduce juvenile delinquency. The District Court also determined that a reasonable observer, mindful of the history, purpose, and context, would not conclude that this passive monument conveyed the message that the State was seeking to endorse religion. The Court of Appeals affirmed the District Court's holdings with respect to the monument's purpose and effect. We . . . affirm.

Our cases, Januslike, point in two directions in applying the Establishment Clause. One face looks toward the strong role played by religion and religious traditions throughout our Nation's history. . . . The other face looks toward the principle that governmental intervention in religious matters can itself endanger religious freedom.

This case, like all Establishment Clause challenges, presents us with the difficulty of respecting both faces. Our institutions presuppose a Supreme Being, yet these institutions must not press religious observances upon their citizens. One face looks to the past in acknowledgment of our Nation's heritage, while the other looks to the present in demanding a separation between church and state. Reconciling these two faces requires that we neither abdicate our responsibility to maintain a division between church and state nor evince a hostility to religion by disabling the government from in some ways recognizing our religious heritage. . . .

These two faces are evident in representative cases both upholding and invalidating laws under the Establishment Clause. Over the last 25 years, we have sometimes pointed to Lemon v. Kurtzman, 403 U.S. 602, (1971), as providing the governing test in Establishment Clause challenges. . . . Others have applied it only after concluding that the challenged practice was invalid under a different Establishment Clause test.

Whatever may be the fate of the *Lemon* test in the larger scheme of Establishment Clause jurisprudence, we think it not useful in dealing with the sort of passive monument that Texas has erected on its Capitol grounds. Instead, our analysis is driven both by the nature of the monument and by our Nation's history.

As we explained in Lynch v. Donnelly, 465 U.S. 668 (1984): "There is an unbroken history of official acknowledgment by all three branches of government of the role of religion in American life from at least 1789" . . . .

Recognition of the role of God in our Nation's heritage has also been reflected in our decisions. . . .

In this case we are faced with a display of the Ten Commandments on government property outside the Texas State Capitol. Such acknowledgments of the role played by the Ten Commandments in our Nation's heritage are common throughout America. We need only look within our own Courtroom. Since 1935, Moses has stood, holding two tablets that reveal portions of the Ten Commandments written in Hebrew, among other lawgivers in the south frieze.

Representations of the Ten Commandments adorn the metal gates lining the north and south sides of the Courtroom as well as the doors leading into the Courtroom. Moses also sits on the exterior east facade of the building holding the Ten Commandments tablets.

Similar acknowledgments can be seen throughout a visitor's tour of our Nation's Capital. . . .

Our opinions, like our building, have recognized the role the Decalogue plays in America's heritage. . . . These displays and recognitions of the Ten Commandments bespeak the rich American tradition of religious acknowledgments.

Of course, the Ten Commandments are religious—they were so viewed at their inception and so remain. The monument, therefore, has religious significance. According to Judeo–Christian belief, the Ten Commandments were given to Moses by God on Mt. Sinai. But Moses was a lawgiver as well as a religious leader. And the Ten Commandments have an undeniable historical meaning, as the foregoing examples demonstrate. Simply having religious content or promoting a message consistent with a religious doctrine does not run afoul of the Establishment Clause. . . .

There are, of course, limits to the display of religious messages or symbols. For example, we held unconstitutional a Kentucky statute requiring the posting of the Ten Commandments in every public schoolroom. Stone v. Graham, 449 U.S. 39 (1980) *(per curiam).* In the classroom context, we found that the Kentucky statute had an improper and plainly religious purpose. . . . As evidenced by *Stone*'s almost exclusive reliance upon two of our school prayer cases, it stands as an example of the fact that we have "been particularly vigilant in monitoring compliance with the Establishment Clause in elementary and secondary schools," . . . . Neither *Stone* itself nor subsequent opinions have indicated that *Stone*'s holding would extend to a legislative chamber, . . . or to capitol grounds.

The placement of the Ten Commandments monument on the Texas State Capitol grounds is a far more passive use of those texts than was the case in *Stone,* where the text confronted elementary school students every day. Indeed, Van Orden, the petitioner here, apparently walked by the monument for a number of years before bringing this lawsuit. . . . Texas has treated her Capitol grounds monuments as representing the several strands in the State's political and legal history. The inclusion of the Ten Commandments monument in this group has a dual significance, partaking of both religion and government. We cannot say that Texas' display of this monument violates the Establishment Clause of the First Amendment.

The judgment of the Court of Appeals is affirmed.

. . .

Justice Scalia, concurring.

I join the opinion of the Chief Justice because I think it accurately reflects our current Establishment Clause jurisprudence—or at least the Establishment Clause jurisprudence we currently apply some of the time. I would prefer to reach the same result by adopting an Establishment Clause jurisprudence that is in accord with our Nation's past and present practices, and that can be consistently applied—the central relevant feature of which is that there is nothing unconstitutional in a State's favoring religion generally, honoring God through public prayer and acknowledgment, or, in a nonproselytizing manner, venerating the Ten Commandments . . .

Justice Thomas, concurring.

. . . I join the Chief Justice's opinion in full.

This case would be easy if the Court were willing to abandon the inconsistent guideposts it has adopted for addressing Establishment Clause challenges, and return to the original meaning of the Clause. I have previously suggested that the Clause's text and history "resis[t] incorporation" against the States. . . . If the Establishment Clause does not restrain the States, then it has no application here, where only state action is at issue.

Even if the Clause is incorporated, or if the Free Exercise Clause limits the power of States to establish religions, . . . our task would be far simpler if we returned to the original meaning of the word "establishment" than it is under the various approaches this Court now uses. The Framers understood an establishment "necessarily [to] involve actual legal coercion." . . .

There is no question that, based on the original meaning of the Establishment Clause, the Ten Commandments display at issue here is constitutional. In no sense does Texas compel petitioner Van Orden to do anything. The only injury to him is that he takes offense at seeing the monument as he passes it on his way to the Texas Supreme Court Library. He need not stop to read it or even to look at it, let alone to express support for it or adopt the Commandments as guides for his life. The mere presence of the monument along his path involves no coercion and thus does not violate the Establishment Clause.

Returning to the original meaning would do more than simplify our task. It also would avoid the pitfalls present in the Court's current approach to such challenges. This Court's precedent elevates the trivial to the proverbial "federal case," by making benign signs and postings subject to challenge. Yet even as it does so, the Court's precedent attempts to avoid declaring all religious symbols and words of longstanding tradition unconstitutional, by counterfactually declaring them of little religious significance. . . .

. . .

[T]he very "flexibility" of this Court's Establishment Clause precedent leaves it incapable of consistent application. . . .

The unintelligibility of this Court's precedent raises the further concern that, either in appearance or in fact, adjudication of Establishment Clause challenges turns on judicial predilections. . . .

Much, if not all, of this would be avoided if the Court would return to the views of the Framers and adopt coercion as the touchstone for our Establishment Clause inquiry. Every acknowledgment of religion would not give rise to an Establishment Clause claim. Courts would not act as theological commissions, judging the meaning of religious matters. Most important, our precedent would be capable of consistent and coherent application. While the Court correctly rejects the challenge to the Ten Commandments monument on the

Texas Capitol grounds, a more fundamental rethinking of our Establishment Clause jurisprudence remains in order.

Justice Breyer, concurring in the judgment.

In School Dist. of Abington Township v. Schempp, 374 U.S. 203 (1963), Justice Goldberg, joined by Justice Harlan, wrote, in respect to the First Amendment's Religion Clauses, that there is "no simple and clear measure which by precise application can readily and invariably demark the permissible from the impermissible." ... One must refer instead to the basic purposes of those Clauses. They seek to "assure the fullest possible scope of religious liberty and tolerance for all." They seek to avoid that divisiveness based upon religion that promotes social conflict, sapping the strength of government and religion alike.... They seek to maintain that "separation of church and state" that has long been critical to the "peaceful dominion that religion exercises in [this] country,"....

. . .

Thus, as Justices Goldberg and Harlan pointed out, the Court has found no single mechanical formula that can accurately draw the constitutional line in every case.... Where the Establishment Clause is at issue, tests designed to measure "neutrality" alone are insufficient, both because it is sometimes difficult to determine when a legal rule is "neutral," and because "untutored devotion to the concept of neutrality can lead to invocation or approval of results which partake not simply of that noninterference and noninvolvement with the religious which the Constitution commands, but of a brooding and pervasive devotion to the secular and a passive, or even active, hostility to the religious." ...

Neither can this Court's other tests readily explain the Establishment Clause's tolerance, for example, of the prayers that open legislative meetings, ... certain references to, and invocations of, the Deity in the public words of public officials; the public references to God on coins, decrees, and buildings; or the attention paid to the religious objectives of certain holidays, including Thanksgiving....

If the relation between government and religion is one of separation, but not of mutual hostility and suspicion, one will inevitably find difficult borderline cases. And in such cases, I see no test-related substitute for the exercise of legal judgment.... That judgment is not a personal judgment. Rather, as in all constitutional cases, it must reflect and remain faithful to the underlying purposes of the Clauses, and it must take account of context and consequences measured in light of those purposes. While the Court's prior tests provide useful guideposts—and might well lead to the same result the Court reaches today.... —no exact formula can dictate a resolution to such fact-intensive cases.

The case before us is a borderline case. It concerns a large granite monument bearing the text of the Ten Commandments located on the grounds of the Texas State Capitol. On the one hand, the Commandments' text undeniably has a religious message, invoking, indeed emphasizing, the Deity. On the other hand, focusing on the text of the Commandments alone cannot conclusively resolve this case. Rather, to determine the message that the text here conveys, we must examine how the text is *used.* And that inquiry requires us to consider the context of the display.

In certain contexts, a display of the tablets of the Ten Commandments can convey not simply a religious message but also a secular moral message (about proper standards of social conduct). And in certain contexts, a display of the tablets can also convey a historical message (about a historic relation between those standards and the law)—a fact that helps to explain the display of those tablets in dozens of courthouses throughout the Nation, including the Supreme Court of the United States. . . .

Here the tablets have been used as part of a display that communicates not simply a religious message, but a secular message as well. The circumstances surrounding the display's placement on the capitol grounds and its physical setting suggest that the State itself intended the latter, nonreligious aspects of the tablets' message to predominate. And the monument's 40-year history on the Texas state grounds indicates that that has been its effect.

The group that donated the monument, the Fraternal Order of Eagles, a private civic (and primarily secular) organization, while interested in the religious aspect of the Ten Commandments, sought to highlight the Commandments' role in shaping civic morality as part of that organization's efforts to combat juvenile delinquency. . . . The Eagles' consultation with a committee composed of members of several faiths in order to find a nonsectarian text underscores the group's ethics-based motives. The tablets, as displayed on the monument, prominently acknowledge that the Eagles donated the display, a factor which, though not sufficient, thereby further distances the State itself from the religious aspect of the Commandments' message.

. . .

. . . As far as I can tell, 40 years passed in which the presence of this monument, legally speaking, went unchallenged (until the single legal objection raised by petitioner). And I am not aware of any evidence suggesting that this was due to a climate of intimidation. Hence, those 40 years suggest more strongly than can any set of formulaic tests that few individuals, whatever their system of beliefs, are likely to have understood the monument as amounting, in any significantly detrimental way, to a government effort to favor a particular religious sect, primarily to promote religion over nonreligion, to "engage in" any "religious practic[e]," to "compel" any "religious practic[e]," or to "work deterrence" of any "religious belief." . . . Those 40 years suggest that the public visiting the capitol grounds has considered the religious aspect of the tablets' message as part of what is a broader moral and historical message reflective of a cultural heritage.

This case, moreover, is distinguishable from instances where the Court has found Ten Commandments displays impermissible. The display is not on the grounds of a public school, where, given the impressionability of the young, government must exercise particular care in separating church and state. . . . This case also differs from *McCreary County*, where the short (and stormy) history of the courthouse Commandments' displays demonstrates the substantially religious objectives of those who mounted them, and the effect of this readily apparent objective upon those who view them. . . . That history there indicates a governmental effort substantially to promote religion, not simply an effort primarily to reflect, historically, the secular impact of a religiously inspired document. And, in today's world, in a Nation of so many different religious and comparable nonreligious fundamental beliefs, a more contemporary state effort to focus attention upon a religious text is certainly likely to prove divisive in a way that this longstanding, pre-existing monument has not.

For these reasons, I believe that the Texas display—serving a mixed but primarily nonreligious purpose, not primarily "advanc[ing]" or "inhibit[ing] religion," and not creating an "excessive government entanglement with religion,"—might satisfy this Court's more formal Establishment Clause tests.... But, as I have said, in reaching the conclusion that the Texas display falls on the permissible side of the constitutional line, I rely less upon a literal application of any particular test than upon consideration of the basic purposes of the First Amendment's Religion Clauses themselves. This display has stood apparently uncontested for nearly two generations. That experience helps us understand that as a practical matter of *degree* this display is unlikely to prove divisive. And this matter of degree is, I believe, critical in a borderline case such as this one.

At the same time, to reach a contrary conclusion here, based primarily upon the religious nature of the tablets' text would, I fear, lead the law to exhibit a hostility toward religion that has no place in our Establishment Clause traditions. Such a holding might well encourage disputes concerning the removal of longstanding depictions of the Ten Commandments from public buildings across the Nation. And it could thereby create the very kind of religiously based divisiveness that the Establishment Clause seeks to avoid....

In light of these considerations, I cannot agree with today's plurality's analysis. Nor can I agree with Justice Scalia's dissent in ... *McCreary County*.... I do agree with Justice O'Connor's statement of principles in *McCreary County*, ... though I disagree with her evaluation of the evidence as it bears on the application of those principles to this case.

I concur in the judgment of the Court.

Justice Stevens, with whom Justice Ginsburg joins, dissenting.

The sole function of the monument on the grounds of Texas' State Capitol is to display the full text of one version of the Ten Commandments. The monument is not a work of art and does not refer to any event in the history of the State....

. . .

As the story goes, the program was initiated by the late Judge E.J. Ruegemer, a Minnesota juvenile court judge and then-Chairman of the Eagles National Commission on Youth Guidance. Inspired by a juvenile offender who had never heard of the Ten Commandments, the judge approached the Minnesota Eagles with the idea of distributing paper copies of the Commandments to be posted in courthouses nationwide. The State's Aerie undertook this project and its popularity spread. When Cecil B. DeMille, who at that time was filming the movie The Ten Commandments, heard of the judge's endeavor, he teamed up with the Eagles to produce the type of granite monolith now displayed in front of the Texas Capitol and at courthouse squares, city halls, and public parks throughout the Nation. Granite was reportedly chosen over DeMille's original suggestion of bronze plaques to better replicate the original Ten Commandments.

The donors were motivated by a desire to "inspire the youth" and curb juvenile delinquency by providing children with a "code of conduct or standards by which to govern their actions." It is the Eagles' belief that disseminating the message conveyed by the Ten Commandments will help to persuade young men and women to observe civilized standards of behavior, and will lead to more productive lives. . . .

The desire to combat juvenile delinquency by providing guidance to youths is both admirable and unquestionably secular. But achieving that goal through biblical teachings injects a religious purpose into an otherwise secular endeavor. By spreading the word of God and converting heathens to Christianity, missionaries expect to enlighten their converts, enhance their satisfaction with life, and improve their behavior. Similarly, by disseminating the "law of God"—directing fidelity to God and proscribing murder, theft, and adultery—the Eagles hope that this divine guidance will help wayward youths conform their behavior and improve their lives. In my judgment, the significant secular by-products that are intended consequences of religious instruction—indeed, of the establishment of most religions—are not the type of "secular" purposes that justify government promulgation of sacred religious messages.

Though the State of Texas may genuinely wish to combat juvenile delinquency, and may rightly want to honor the Eagles for their efforts, it cannot effectuate these admirable purposes through an explicitly religious medium. . . . The State may admonish its citizens not to lie, cheat or steal, to honor their parents and to respect their neighbors' property; and it may do so by printed words, in television commercials, or on granite monuments in front of its public buildings. Moreover, the State may provide its schoolchildren and adult citizens with educational materials that explain the important role that our forebears' faith in God played in their decisions to select America as a refuge from religious persecution, to declare their independence from the British Crown, and to conceive a new Nation. . . . The message at issue in this case, however, is fundamentally different from either a bland admonition to observe generally accepted rules of behavior or a general history lesson.

The reason this message stands apart is that the Decalogue is a venerable religious text. . . . Thankfully, the plurality does not attempt to minimize the religious significance of the Ten Commandments. . . . Attempts to secularize what is unquestionably a sacred text defy credibility and disserve people of faith.

The profoundly sacred message embodied by the text inscribed on the Texas monument is emphasized by the especially large letters that identify its author: "**I AM the LORD thy God.**" . . . It commands present worship of Him and no other deity. It directs us to be guided by His teaching in the current and future conduct of all of our affairs. It instructs us to follow a code of divine law, some of which has informed and been integrated into our secular legal code ("Thou shalt not kill"), but much of which has not ("Thou shalt not make to thyself any graven images. . . . Thou shalt not covet").

Moreover, despite the Eagles' best efforts to choose a benign nondenominational text, the Ten Commandments display projects not just a religious, but an inherently sectarian message. There are many distinctive versions of the Decalogue, ascribed to by different religions and even different denominations within a particular faith; to a pious and learned observer, these differences may be of enormous religious significance. . . .

Even if, however, the message of the monument, despite the inscribed text, fairly could be said to represent the belief system of all Judeo-Christians, it would still run afoul of the Establishment Clause by prescribing a compelled code of conduct from one God, namely a Judeo–Christian God, that is rejected by prominent polytheistic sects, such as Hinduism, as well as nontheistic religions, such as Buddhism. . . . Any of those bases, in my judgment, would be sufficient to conclude that the message should not be proclaimed by the State of Texas on a permanent monument at the seat of its government.

. . .

Recognizing the diversity of religious and secular beliefs held by Texans and by all Americans, it seems beyond peradventure that allowing the seat of government to serve as a stage for the propagation of an unmistakably Judeo-Christian message of piety would have the tendency to make nonmonotheists and nonbelievers "feel like [outsiders] in matters of faith, and [strangers] in the political community." . . .

. . .

Critical examination of the Decalogue's prominent display at the seat of Texas government, rather than generic citation to the role of religion in American life, unmistakably reveals on which side of the "slippery slope" this display must fall. God, as the author of its message, the Eagles, as the donor of the monument, and the State of Texas, as its proud owner, speak with one voice for a common purpose—to encourage Texans to abide by the divine code of a "Judeo–Christian" God. If this message is permissible, then the shining principle of neutrality to which we have long adhered is nothing more than mere shadow.

III

The plurality relies heavily on the fact that our Republic was founded, and has been governed since its nascence, by leaders who spoke then (and speak still) in plainly religious rhetoric. . . .

The speeches and rhetoric characteristic of the founding era, however, do not answer the question before us. I have already explained why Texas' display of the full text of the Ten Commandments, given the content of the actual display and the context in which it is situated, sets this case apart from the countless examples of benign government recognitions of religion. But there is another crucial difference. Our leaders, when delivering public addresses, often express their blessings simultaneously in the service of God and their constituents. Thus, when public officials deliver public speeches, we recognize that their words are not exclusively a transmission from *the* government because those oratories have embedded within them the inherently personal views of the speaker as an individual member of the polity. The permanent placement of a textual religious display on state property is different in kind; it amalgamates otherwise discordant individual views into a collective statement of government approval. Moreover, the message never ceases to transmit itself to objecting viewers whose only choices are to accept the message or to ignore the offense by averting their gaze.

The plurality's reliance on early religious statements and proclamations made by the Founders is also problematic because those views were not espoused at the Constitutional Convention in 1787 nor enshrined in the Constitution's text. Thus, the presentation of these religious statements as a unified historical narrative is bound to paint a misleading picture. . . .

. . .

Ardent separationists aside, there is another critical nuance lost in the plurality's portrayal of history. Simply put, many of the Founders who are often cited as authoritative expositors of the Constitution's original meaning understood the Establishment Clause to stand for a *narrower* proposition than the plurality, for whatever reason, is willing to accept. Namely, many of the Framers understood the word "religion" in the Establishment Clause to encompass only the various sects of Christianity.

. . .

Unless one is willing to renounce over 65 years of Establishment Clause jurisprudence and cross back over the incorporation bridge, . . . appeals to the religiosity of the Framers ring hollow. But even if there were a coherent way to embrace incorporation with one hand while steadfastly abiding by the Founders' purported religious views on the other, the problem of the selective use of history remains. As the widely divergent views espoused by the leaders of our founding era plainly reveal, the historical record of the preincorporation Establishment Clause is too indeterminate to serve as an interpretive North Star.

It is our duty, therefore, to interpret the First Amendment's command that "Congress shall make no law respecting an establishment of religion" not by merely asking what those words meant to observers at the time of the founding, but instead by deriving from the Clause's text and history the broad principles that remain valid today. To reason from the broad principles contained in the Constitution does not, as Justice Scalia suggests, require us to abandon our heritage in favor of unprincipled expressions of personal preference. The task of applying the broad principles that the Framers wrote into the text of the First Amendment is, in any event, no more a matter of personal preference than is one's selection between two (or more) sides in a heated historical debate. We serve our constitutional mandate by expounding the meaning of constitutional provisions with one eye towards our Nation's history and the other fixed on its democratic aspirations. . . .

The principle that guides my analysis is neutrality. The basis for that principle is firmly rooted in our Nation's history and our Constitution's text. I recognize that the requirement that government must remain neutral between religion and irreligion would have seemed foreign to some of the Framers; so too would a requirement of neutrality between Jews and Christians. . . . The evil of discriminating today against atheists, "polytheists[,] and believers in unconcerned deities," *McCreary County*, . . . (Scalia, J., dissenting), is in my view a direct descendent of the evil of discriminating among Christian sects.

The Establishment Clause thus forbids it and, in turn, forbids Texas from displaying the Ten Commandments monument the plurality so casually affirms.

IV

The Eagles may donate as many monuments as they choose to be displayed in front of Protestant churches, benevolent organizations' meeting places, or on the front lawns of private citizens. The expurgated text of the King James version of the Ten Commandments that they have crafted is unlikely to be accepted by Catholic parishes, Jewish synagogues, or even some Protestant denominations, but the message they seek to convey is surely more compatible with church property than with property that is located on the government side of the metaphorical wall.

The judgment of the Court in this case stands for the proposition that the Constitution permits governmental displays of sacred religious texts. This makes a mockery of the constitutional ideal that government must remain neutral between religion and irreligion. If a State may endorse a particular deity's command to "have no other gods before me," it is difficult to conceive of any textual display that would run afoul of the Establishment Clause.

The disconnect between this Court's approval of Texas's monument and the constitutional prohibition against preferring religion to irreligion cannot be reduced to the exercise of plotting two adjacent locations on a slippery slope.... Rather, it is the difference between the shelter of a fortress and exposure to "the winds that would blow" if the wall were allowed to crumble.... That wall, however imperfect, remains worth preserving.

I respectfully dissent.

Justice O'Connor, dissenting.

For essentially the reasons given by Justice Souter, as well as the reasons given in my concurrence in McCreary County v. American Civil Liberties Union of Ky., I respectfully dissent.

Justice Souter, with whom Justice Stevens and Justice Ginsburg join, dissenting.

Although the First Amendment's Religion Clauses have not been read to mandate absolute governmental neutrality toward religion, ... the Establishment Clause requires neutrality as a general rule.... A governmental display of an obviously religious text cannot be squared with neutrality, except in a setting that plausibly indicates that the statement is not placed in view with a predominant purpose on the part of government either to adopt the religious message or to urge its acceptance by others.

Until today, only one of our cases addressed the constitutionality of posting the Ten Commandments, Stone v. Graham, 449 U.S. 39, 41–42 (1980) *(per curiam)*. A Kentucky statute required posting the Commandments on the walls of public school classrooms, and the Court described the State's purpose (relevant under the tripartite test laid out in Lemon v. Kurtzman ...) as being at odds with the obligation of religious neutrality.

. . .

What these observations underscore are the simple realities that the Ten Commandments constitute a religious statement, that their message is inherently religious, and that the purpose of singling them out in a display is clearly the same.

Thus, a pedestrian happening upon the monument at issue here needs no training in religious doctrine to realize that the statement of the Commandments, quoting God himself, proclaims that the will of the divine being is the source of obligation to obey the rules, including the facially secular ones. In this case, moreover, the text is presented to give particular prominence to the Commandments' first sectarian reference, "I am the Lord thy God." That proclamation is centered on the stone and written in slightly larger letters than the subsequent recitation. To ensure that the religious nature of the monument is clear to even the most casual passerby, the word "Lord" appears in all capital letters (as does the word "am"), so that the most eye-catching segment of the quotation is the declaration "I AM the LORD thy God." What follows, of course, are the rules against other gods, graven images, vain swearing, and Sabbath breaking. And the full text of the fifth Commandment puts forward filial respect as a condition of long life in the land "which the Lord they God giveth thee." . . .

To drive the religious point home, and identify the message as religious to any viewer who failed to read the text, the engraved quotation is framed by religious symbols: two tablets with what appears to be ancient script on them, two Stars of David, and the superimposed Greek letters Chi and Rho as the familiar monogram of Christ. Nothing on the monument, in fact, detracts from its religious nature. . . .

The monument's presentation of the Commandments with religious text emphasized and enhanced stands in contrast to any number of perfectly constitutional depictions of them, the frieze of our own Courtroom providing a good example, where the figure of Moses stands among history's great lawgivers. While Moses holds the tablets of the Commandments showing some Hebrew text, no one looking at the lines of figures in marble relief is likely to see a religious purpose behind the assemblage or take away a religious message from it. Only one other depiction represents a religious leader, and the historical personages are mixed with symbols of moral and intellectual abstractions like Equity and Authority. . . .

Texas seeks to take advantage of the recognition that visual symbol and written text can manifest a secular purpose in secular company, when it argues that its monument (like Moses in the frieze) is not alone and ought to be viewed as only 1 among 17 placed on the 22 acres surrounding the state capitol. Texas, indeed, says that the Capitol grounds are like a museum for a collection of exhibits, the kind of setting that several Members of the Court have said can render the exhibition of religious artifacts permissible, even though in other circumstances their display would be seen as meant to convey a religious message forbidden to the State. . . . So, for example, the Government of the United States does not violate the Establishment Clause by hanging Giotto's Madonna on the wall of the National Gallery.

But 17 monuments with no common appearance, history, or esthetic role scattered over 22 acres is not a museum, and anyone strolling around the lawn would surely take each memorial on its own terms without any dawning sense that some purpose held the miscellany together more coherently than fortuity and the edge of the grass. One monument expresses admiration for pioneer women. One pays respect to the fighters of World War II. And one quotes the God of Abraham whose command is the sanction for moral law. The themes are individual grit, patriotic courage, and God as the source of Jewish and Christian morality; there is no common denominator....

. . .

Finally, though this too is a point on which judgment will vary, I do not see a persuasive argument for constitutionality in the plurality's observation that Van Orden's lawsuit comes "[f]orty years after the monument's erection ... ," an observation that echoes the State's contention that one fact cutting in its favor is that "the monument stood ... in Austin ... for some forty years without generating any controversy or litigation," .... It is not that I think the passage of time is necessarily irrelevant in Establishment Clause analysis. We have approved framing-era practices because they must originally have been understood as constitutionally permissible, ... and we have recognized that Sunday laws have grown recognizably secular over time.... There is also an analogous argument, not yet evaluated, that ritualistic religious expression can become so numbing over time that its initial Establishment Clause violation becomes at some point too diminished for notice. But I do not understand any of these to be the State's argument, which rather seems to be that 40 years without a challenge shows that as a factual matter the religious expression is too tepid to provoke a serious reaction and constitute a violation. Perhaps, but the writer of Exodus chapter 20 was not lukewarm, and other explanations may do better in accounting for the late resort to the courts. Suing a State over religion puts nothing in a plaintiff's pocket and can take a great deal out, and even with volunteer litigators to supply time and energy, the risk of social ostracism can be powerfully deterrent. I doubt that a slow walk to the courthouse, even one that took 40 years, is much evidentiary help in applying the Establishment Clause.

I would reverse the judgment of the Court of Appeals.

SECTION 2. THE FREE EXERCISE OF RELIGION

Page 1845. Add at end of chapter:

Cutter v. Wilkinson

___ U.S. ___, 125 S.Ct. 2113, ___ L.Ed.2d ___ (2005).

Justice Ginsburg delivered the opinion of the Court.

Section 3 of the Religious Land Use and Institutionalized Persons Act of 2000 (RLUIPA), 114 Stat. 804, provides in part: "No government shall impose a substantial burden on the religious exercise of a person residing in or confined to an institution," unless the burden furthers "a compelling governmental interest," and does so by "the least restrictive means." Plaintiffs below, petitioners here, are current and former inmates of institutions operated by the

Ohio Department of Rehabilitation and Correction and assert that they are adherents of "nonmainstream" religions: the Satanist, Wicca, and Asatru religions, and the Church of Jesus Christ Christian. They complain that Ohio prison officials (respondents here), in violation of RLUIPA, have failed to accommodate their religious exercise "in a variety of different ways, including retaliating and discriminating against them for exercising their nontraditional faiths, denying them access to religious literature, denying them the same opportunities for group worship that are granted to adherents of mainstream religions, forbidding them to adhere to the dress and appearance mandates of their religions, withholding religious ceremonial items that are substantially identical to those that the adherents of mainstream religions are permitted, and failing to provide a chaplain trained in their faith." ...

In response to petitioners' complaints, respondent prison officials have mounted a facial challenge to the institutionalized-persons provision of RLUIPA; respondents contend, *inter alia*, that the Act improperly advances religion in violation of the First Amendment's Establishment Clause. The District Court denied respondents' motion to dismiss petitioners' complaints, but the Court of Appeals reversed that determination. The appeals court held, as the prison officials urged, that the portion of RLUIPA applicable to institutionalized persons ... violates the Establishment Clause. We reverse the Court of Appeals' judgment.

"This Court has long recognized that the government may ... accommodate religious practices ... without violating the Establishment Clause." ... § 3 of RLUIPA, we hold, does not, on its face, exceed the limits of permissible government accommodation of religious practices.

I

A

RLUIPA is the latest of long-running congressional efforts to accord religious exercise heightened protection from government-imposed burdens, consistent with this Court's precedents. Ten years before RLUIPA's enactment, the Court held, in Employment Div., Dept. of Human Resources of Ore. v. Smith, ... that the First Amendment's Free Exercise Clause does not inhibit enforcement of otherwise valid laws of general application that incidentally burden religious conduct. In particular, we ruled that the Free Exercise Clause did not bar Oregon from enforcing its blanket ban on peyote possession with no allowance for sacramental use of the drug. Accordingly, the State could deny unemployment benefits to persons dismissed from their jobs because of their religiously inspired peyote use. The Court recognized, however, that the political branches could shield religious exercise through legislative accommodation, for example, by making an exception to proscriptive drug laws for sacramental peyote use....

Responding to *Smith*, Congress enacted the Religious Freedom Restoration Act of 1993 (RFRA).... In *City of Boerne*, this Court invalidated RFRA as applied to States and their subdivisions, holding that the Act exceeded Congress' remedial powers under the Fourteenth Amendment.[2] ... Congress again

2. RFRA, Courts of Appeals have held, remains operative as to the Federal Government and federal territories and possessions.... This Court, however, has not had occasion to rule on the matter.

responded, this time by enacting RLUIPA. Less sweeping than RFRA, and invoking federal authority under the Spending and Commerce Clauses, RLUIPA targets two areas: Section 2 of the Act concerns land-use regulation . . .; § 3 relates to religious exercise by institutionalized persons. . . . Section 3, at issue here, provides that "[n]o [state or local] government shall impose a substantial burden on the religious exercise of a person residing in or confined to an institution," unless the government shows that the burden furthers "a compelling governmental interest" and does so by "the least restrictive means." . . . The Act defines "religious exercise" to include "any exercise of religion, whether or not compelled by, or central to, a system of religious belief." . . . Section 3 applies when "the substantial burden [on religious exercise] is imposed in a program or activity that receives Federal financial assistance," or "the substantial burden affects, or removal of that substantial burden would affect, commerce with foreign nations, among the several States, or with Indian tribes." . . . "A person may assert a violation of [RLUIPA] as a claim or defense in a judicial proceeding and obtain appropriate relief against a government." . . .

Before enacting § 3, Congress documented, in hearings spanning three years, that "frivolous or arbitrary" barriers impeded institutionalized persons' religious exercise. . . . To secure redress for inmates who encountered undue barriers to their religious observances, Congress carried over from RFRA the "compelling governmental interest"/"least restrictive means" standard. . . .

B

Petitioners initially filed suit against respondents asserting claims under the First and Fourteenth Amendments. After RLUIPA's enactment, petitioners amended their complaints to include claims under § 3. Respondents moved to dismiss the statutory claims. . . .

. . . [T]he District Court rejected the argument that § 3 conflicts with the Establishment Clause. . . .

. . . [T]he Court of Appeals for the Sixth Circuit reversed[, . . . holding] that § 3 of RLUIPA "impermissibly advanc[es] religion by giving greater protection to religious rights than to other constitutionally protected rights." . . . Affording "religious prisoners rights superior to those of nonreligious prisoners," the court suggested, might "encourag[e] prisoners to become religious in order to enjoy greater rights." . . .

We granted certiorari to resolve the conflict among Courts of Appeals on the question whether RLUIPA's institutionalized-persons provision, § 3 of the Act, is consistent with the Establishment Clause of the First Amendment. . . . We now reverse the judgment of the Court of Appeals for the Sixth Circuit.

II

A

. . . While the two [Religion] Clauses express complementary values, they often exert conflicting pressures. *See* . . . *Walz* . . . ("The Court has struggled to find a neutral course between the two Religion Clauses, both of which are cast in absolute terms, and either of which, if expanded to a logical extreme, would tend to clash with the other.").

Our decisions recognize that "there is room for play in the joints" between the Clauses, ... some space for legislative action neither compelled by the Free Exercise Clause nor prohibited by the Establishment Clause.... On its face, the Act qualifies as a permissible legislative accommodation of religion that is not barred by the Establishment Clause.

Foremost, we find RLUIPA's institutionalized-persons provision compatible with the Establishment Clause because it alleviates exceptional government-created burdens on private religious exercise.... Furthermore, the Act on its face does not founder on shoals our prior decisions have identified: Properly applying RLUIPA, courts must take adequate account of the burdens a requested accommodation may impose on nonbeneficiaries ... and they must be satisfied that the Act's prescriptions are and will be administered neutrally among different faiths....

... Section 3 covers state-run institutions—mental hospitals, prisons, and the like—in which the government exerts a degree of control unparalleled in civilian society and severely disabling to private religious exercise.... RLUIPA thus protects institutionalized persons who are unable freely to attend to their religious needs and are therefore dependent on the government's permission and accommodation for exercise of their religion.

... In *Goldman v. Weinberger*, 475 U.S. 503, we held that the Free Exercise Clause did not require the Air Force to exempt an Orthodox Jewish officer from uniform dress regulations so that he could wear a yarmulke indoors. In a military community, the Court observed, "there is simply not the same [individual] autonomy as there is in the larger civilian community." ... Congress responded to *Goldman* by prescribing that "a member of the armed forces may wear an item of religious apparel while wearing the uniform," unless "the wearing of the item would interfere with the performance [of] military duties [or] the item of apparel is not neat and conservative." ...

We do not read RLUIPA to elevate accommodation of religious observances over an institution's need to maintain order and safety. Our decisions indicate that an accommodation must be measured so that it does not override other significant interests. In *Caldor*, the Court struck down a Connecticut law that "arm[ed] Sabbath observers with an absolute and unqualified right not to work on whatever day they designate[d] as their Sabbath." ... We held the law invalid under the Establishment Clause because it "unyielding[ly] weigh[ted]" the interests of Sabbatarians "over all other interests." ...

We have no cause to believe that RLUIPA would not be applied in an appropriately balanced way, with particular sensitivity to security concerns. While the Act adopts a "compelling governmental interest" standard, ... [l]awmakers supporting RLUIPA were mindful of the urgency of discipline, order, safety, and security in penal institutions....

. . .

B

The Sixth Circuit misread our precedents to require invalidation of RLUIPA as "impermissibly advancing religion by giving greater protection to religious rights than to other constitutionally protected rights." . . . Our decision in *Amos* counsels otherwise. There, we upheld against an Establishment Clause challenge a provision exempting "religious organizations from Title VII's prohibition against discrimination in employment on the basis of religion." . . . Religious accommodations, we held, need not "come packaged with benefits to secular entities." . . .

Were the Court of Appeals' view the correct reading of our decisions, all manner of religious accommodations would fall. Congressional permission for members of the military to wear religious apparel while in uniform would fail. . . . Ohio could not, as it now does, accommodate "traditionally recognized" religions . . . : The State provides inmates with chaplains "but not with publicists or political consultants," and allows "prisoners to assemble for worship, but not for political rallies."

In upholding RLUIPA's institutionalized-persons provision, we emphasize that respondents "have raised a facial challenge to [the Act's] constitutionality, and have not contended that under the facts of any of [petitioners'] specific cases . . . [that] applying RLUIPA would produce unconstitutional results." . . .

. . .

Justice Thomas, concurring.

I join the opinion of the Court. I agree with the Court that the Religious Land Use and Institutionalized Persons Act of 2000 (RLUIPA) is constitutional under our modern Establishment Clause case law. I write to explain why a proper historical understanding of the Clause as a federalism provision leads to the same conclusion.

. . .

†